RHODES

TRAVEL GUIDE

Discovering the Charm of Rhodes, Greece: A Destination for Adventure, Culture and Beauty

NICHOLAS Z. ANDREW

TABLE OF CONTENTS

CHAPTER ONE

WELCOME TO RHODES

Rhodes is the largest of the Dodecanese Islands in Greece and is known for its stunning beaches, ancient history, and rich culture. The island is located in the southeastern Aegean Sea, close to Turkey, and has been inhabited since the Neolithic period.

Brief History Of Rhodes

Rhodes has a rich and diverse history, dating back to the Neolithic period. The island's strategic location in the eastern Mediterranean has made it a coveted prize for many civilizations throughout history, including the Greeks, Romans, Byzantines, Knights of St. John, Ottomans, and Italians.

Ancient History
The ancient history of Rhodes is rich and fascinating, with evidence of human settlement on the island dating back to the Neolithic period. The island's strategic location in the eastern Mediterranean has made it a center of trade and commerce throughout history, and it has been inhabited by various civilizations over the centuries.

Minoan and Mycenaean Periods

The Minoans were the first significant civilization to inhabit Rhodes, arriving on the island around 1600 BC. They established a flourishing culture, with evidence of their pottery, tools, and jewelry still visible on the island today. The Mycenaeans later established a colony on Rhodes in the 15th century BC, and they built the Acropolis of Lindos, one of the island's most famous ancient sites.

Classical Period

In the 5th century BC, Rhodes became part of the Athenian empire, but it gained independence in 408 BC and established its own democratic government. During this time, Rhodes became a major center for trade and commerce, with its ships sailing as far as India and Egypt. The island was also home to the famous Colossus of Rhodes, a statue of the Greek god Helios that stood at the entrance to the harbor. The statue was one of the Seven Wonders of the Ancient World and was destroyed by an earthquake in 226 BC.

Hellenistic Period

Rhodes reached the height of its power and influence during the Hellenistic period, when it became the center of the Rhodian maritime empire. The Rhodians established a powerful navy and controlled a vast trade network that spanned the Mediterranean. The island was also home to the famous School of Rhetoric, which was founded by the philosopher and orator, Isocrates.

Roman and Byzantine Periods
Rhodes became part of the Roman Empire in 43 BC and remained under Roman rule for almost 500 years. During this time, the island was a popular destination for wealthy Romans, who built luxurious villas and bathhouses. Rhodes also became an important center for Christianity during the Byzantine period, and many churches and monasteries were built on the island during this time.

Overall, the ancient history of Rhodes is a testament to the island's rich cultural heritage, and the ruins and monuments that remain today are a fascinating glimpse into the island's past.

Medieval History
During the medieval period, Rhodes was an important center of power and commerce, serving as a key link between the East and the West. The island's strategic location made it a coveted prize for many civilizations, and it was ruled by various powers throughout the centuries.

The Knights of St. John
In 1309, the Knights of St. John, a Catholic military order, conquered Rhodes and established a new capital city on the site of the ancient Acropolis. The

order was dedicated to protecting pilgrims traveling to the Holy Land, and they quickly established a powerful presence in Rhodes, building an extensive network of fortifications and defensive structures.

Under the Knights' rule, Rhodes flourished as a center of commerce and culture. The city of Rhodes became a hub for trade between Europe, the Middle East, and Africa, and it was home to a diverse community of merchants, artisans, and scholars.

The Ottomans
Despite the Knights' efforts, Rhodes was eventually conquered by the Ottomans in 1522, following a six-month siege. The Ottoman Empire was a powerful force in the Mediterranean world, and their conquest of Rhodes marked a significant turning point in the island's history.

Under Ottoman rule, Rhodes underwent significant changes. The island's population became predominantly Muslim, and many of the island's churches and Christian institutions were converted into mosques and madrasas. The Ottomans also made significant changes to the island's architecture, introducing new building styles and techniques that were influenced by Islamic and Byzantine traditions.

Despite these changes, Rhodes continued to be an important center of trade and commerce throughout the Ottoman period. The island's port was a key link in the Ottoman trading network, and it was home to a thriving community of merchants and artisans.

The Italian Occupation
In 1912, Rhodes was occupied by the Italians, who established a new government on the island. The Italians invested heavily in the island's infrastructure, building roads, harbors, and public buildings, and also restoring many of the island's ancient monuments.

During World War II, Rhodes was occupied by the Germans, and the island's Jewish population was sent to concentration camps. After the war, Rhodes was returned to Greece, and the island has since become a popular tourist destination, known for its beautiful beaches, rich history, and vibrant culture. The legacy of the Knights of St. John, the Ottomans, and the Italians can still be seen in the island's architecture, art, and culture, making Rhodes a truly unique and fascinating destination.

Modern History
In 1912, Rhodes was occupied by Italy during the Italo-Turkish War, and the island was ceded to Italy under the Treaty of Lausanne in 1923. The Italians established a new government and invested heavily in the island's infrastructure, building roads, harbors, and public buildings, and restoring many of the island's ancient monuments.

During World War II, Rhodes was occupied by the Germans, who replaced the Italian governor with a military commander. The Germans constructed fortifications on the island, including bunkers, anti-aircraft guns, and minefields, in anticipation of an Allied invasion. In 1944, the island was heavily bombed by the Allies, causing extensive damage to the city of Rhodes and the surrounding area. The island's Jewish population was also deported to concentration camps, and very few survived.

After the war, Rhodes was returned to Greece, and the island underwent a period of reconstruction and development. The Greek government invested in the island's infrastructure, building new roads, schools, hospitals, and public buildings, and also established a tourist industry to boost the island's economy.

Today, Rhodes is a popular tourist destination, attracting millions of visitors every year. The island's rich history and cultural heritage are major draws for tourists, and the city of Rhodes has been designated a UNESCO World Heritage Site. The island's beautiful beaches, crystal-clear waters, and stunning natural scenery also make it a popular destination for sun-seekers and outdoor enthusiasts. In recent years, Rhodes has become known for its luxury resorts, spa hotels, and high-end restaurants, as well as its vibrant nightlife scene.

Geography And Location Of Rhodes

Geography

Rhodes is a volcanic island that was formed over millions of years due to volcanic activity. It is part of the South Aegean volcanic arc, which also includes the islands of Santorini and Milos. The island's rugged topography is the result of tectonic activity and erosion over time, which has created a landscape of steep mountains, deep valleys, and dramatic cliffs. The island is also home to several natural springs, which provide a source of fresh water for its inhabitants.

The coastal areas of Rhodes are characterized by beautiful sandy beaches, rocky coves, and crystal-clear waters. The island has a long and diverse coastline that offers something for everyone, from secluded beaches to bustling tourist resorts. Some of the most popular beaches on the island include Faliraki, Lindos, and Tsambika.

Location

Rhodes is located in the southeastern Aegean Sea, close to the coast of Turkey. Its location has made it a strategic location for trade and commerce throughout history, as it lies at the crossroads between Europe, Africa, and Asia. The island is situated at the entrance of the Aegean Sea and is surrounded by several smaller islands and islets, which provide shelter and protection from the open sea.

Rhodes is the largest of the Dodecanese Islands, which are a group of 15 islands and islets located in the eastern Aegean Sea. The other islands in the group include Kos, Patmos, Kalymnos, Leros, Astypalea, and several others. The Dodecanese Islands are known for their rich history, stunning beaches, and unique culture.

Today, Rhodes is a popular tourist destination that attracts visitors from all over the world. Its natural beauty, rich history, and warm hospitality make it an ideal place to relax, explore, and enjoy the Mediterranean lifestyle. Whether you're interested in ancient history, outdoor adventure, or simply soaking up the sun on the beach, Rhodes has something for everyone.

Weather And Climate

Rhodes has a Mediterranean climate with mild, wet winters and hot, dry summers. The island is blessed with plenty of sunshine throughout the year, making it an ideal destination for sun-seekers.

Summer Weather

Rhodes experiences a hot and dry summer season, with an average temperature of 26°C (79°F) in June and July, rising to 27°C (81°F) in August. The hottest month is usually August, with temperatures reaching up to 35°C (95°F) on some days. The sea temperature is also warm during this time, averaging around 25°C (77°F), making it perfect for swimming and other water activities. Due to the high temperatures and sunny weather, summer is the busiest tourist season in Rhodes.

Autumn Weather
Autumn in Rhodes is a great time to visit for those looking for a quieter, more relaxed vacation. The temperatures are still warm, with an average high of around 25°C (77°F) in October, dropping to around 20°C (68°F) in November. The sea temperature remains warm in the autumn months, making it possible to swim in the sea until late October. There may be occasional rainy days, but overall, the weather is mild and comfortable for outdoor activities.

Winter Weather
Winter in Rhodes is mild compared to other parts of Europe, with average temperatures rarely dropping below 10°C (50°F). The wet season in Rhodes is typically between November and March, with occasional storms and heavy rainfall. January and February are the coldest months, with average high temperatures around 15°C (59°F). Many hotels and

restaurants close during the winter months, but if you're interested in exploring the island's cultural sites or hiking in the interior, this can be a great time to visit.

Spring Weather
Spring is a beautiful season in Rhodes, with wildflowers blooming and the countryside coming to life. The temperatures are mild, with an average high of around 20°C (68°F) in March, rising to around 25°C (77°F) in May. There may be occasional showers, but overall, the weather is pleasant and perfect for outdoor activities such as hiking and sightseeing. The sea temperature begins to warm up in April and May, making it possible to swim in the sea by late May.

Overall, Rhodes has a great climate with mild winters and hot summers, and an abundance of sunshine throughout the year. Whether you prefer to visit during the peak tourist season or during the quieter off-season months, there is never a bad time to visit this beautiful island.

Why Visit Rhodes?

Rhodes is a popular tourist destination for many reasons, and it offers a unique blend of history, culture, nature, and relaxation that appeals to a wide variety of travelers. Whether you're interested in exploring ancient ruins, soaking up the sun on a beautiful beach, or experiencing traditional Greek culture, Rhodes has something for everyone. Here are some of the top reasons to visit Rhodes:

History
Rhodes has a rich and diverse history that spans thousands of years. The island was first inhabited during the Neolithic period, and it has been ruled by various civilizations throughout its history, including the Greeks, Romans, Byzantines, Knights of St. John, Ottomans, and Italians. The island's strategic location made it a hub of trade and commerce, and its ancient ruins, medieval Old Town, and Ottoman-era buildings are a testament to its fascinating history. Visitors can explore the ancient ruins of the Acropolis of Rhodes, the Temple of Apollo, and the ancient city of Kamiros, among others.

Beaches
Rhodes is renowned for its stunning beaches, which are among the best in Greece. The island boasts over 30 beaches, ranging from secluded coves to long stretches of sandy shorelines. The crystal-clear waters are perfect for swimming, snorkeling, and other water activities, and the scenery is simply breathtaking. Some of the most popular beaches include Faliraki Beach, Lindos Beach, and Tsambika Beach.

Nature

Rhodes is a paradise for nature lovers, with diverse landscapes ranging from lush green forests to rugged coastline and rocky cliffs. The island's interior is home to stunning natural attractions such as the Valley of the Butterflies, the Seven Springs, and the Profitis Ilias Mountain. Visitors can hike through scenic trails, bike along picturesque routes, or simply enjoy the natural beauty of the island.

Culture

Rhodes has a rich cultural heritage that is celebrated throughout the year with festivals, music, dance, and traditional cuisine. Visitors can experience the local culture by attending festivals such as the Medieval Rose Festival, the Wine Festival, and the traditional Greek Carnival. They can also enjoy traditional music and dance performances, sample local cuisine, and explore the island's museums and galleries.

Nightlife

Rhodes has a vibrant nightlife scene that caters to a variety of tastes and preferences. From laid-back beach bars to high-energy nightclubs, there is something for everyone. The island's nightlife hotspots are concentrated in Faliraki and the Old Town, where visitors can enjoy live music, dancing, and socializing until the early hours of the morning.

In all, Rhodes is a destination that offers a unique blend of history, culture, nature, and relaxation that appeals to a wide variety of travelers. Whether you're interested in exploring ancient ruins, soaking up the sun on a beautiful beach, or experiencing traditional Greek culture, Rhodes has something for everyone.

Best Time To Visit Rhodes

Rhodes is a beautiful island in Greece that attracts tourists from all over the world. The island has a Mediterranean climate with long, hot summers and mild winters. The best time to visit Rhodes depends on your preferences, but generally, the island is best visited from May to October.

Summer Season (June-August)
The summer season in Rhodes is from June to August, and it is the peak tourist season. The weather is hot and sunny, and the sea is perfect for swimming. This is the best time to visit if you are looking for a beach holiday or want to experience the island's vibrant nightlife. However, keep in mind that the island can be crowded during this time, and prices are at their highest.

Shoulder Season (May, September, and October)
The shoulder season in Rhodes is from May to October, excluding the peak months of June to August. The weather is still warm and sunny, but the crowds are thinner, and prices are lower. This is

a great time to visit if you want to enjoy the beaches without the crowds or explore the island's historical and cultural sites. In May, the island is especially beautiful with wildflowers in bloom.

Winter Season (November-April)
The winter season in Rhodes is from November to April. The weather is mild and rainy, and the island is much quieter. This is a good time to visit if you are interested in hiking or exploring the island's cultural sites, as the crowds are thin, and the weather is comfortable for outdoor activities. Keep in mind that many hotels and restaurants close during the winter months, so it's important to check ahead before you go.

Overall, the best time to visit Rhodes depends on your preferences. If you want to experience the island's vibrant nightlife and enjoy a beach holiday, visit during the summer months. If you prefer to avoid the crowds and enjoy a more relaxed atmosphere, visit during the shoulder season. If you are interested in hiking or exploring the island's cultural sites, visit during the winter season.

Essential Things To Pack On Your Rhodes Trip

When planning a trip to Rhodes, packing the right items can make a big difference in your comfort and enjoyment. In this chapter, we will discuss the essential things you should pack on your Rhodes trip as a visitor or tourist.

Comfortable walking shoes

Rhodes is a great place to explore on foot, with many historic sites and attractions located within walking distance of each other. It's important to pack comfortable walking shoes to ensure you can explore the island without discomfort or blisters.

Sun protection

Rhodes has a Mediterranean climate, which means it can get very hot and sunny, especially during the summer months. It's important to pack sun protection such as sunscreen, a hat, and sunglasses to protect yourself from the sun's harmful rays.

Lightweight clothing

To stay cool and comfortable in the hot Rhodes weather, it's important to pack lightweight clothing such as cotton or linen shirts, shorts, and dresses. It's also a good idea to pack a light jacket or sweater for cooler evenings or air-conditioned spaces.

Beachwear

Rhodes has many beautiful beaches, so it's important to pack appropriate beachwear such as swimsuits, cover-ups, and beach towels. It's also a good idea to pack a waterproof bag or pouch to protect your phone and other valuables from water damage.

Travel adapter

Greece uses the European plug type, so if you're traveling from a country that uses a different plug type, it's important to pack a travel adapter to ensure you can charge your electronics.

Medications and first aid kit

If you require any medications or have any medical conditions, it's important to pack enough medication to last your entire trip. It's also a good idea to pack a small first aid kit with essentials such as bandages, antiseptic wipes, and pain relief medication.

Cash and credit cards

While many places in Rhodes accept credit cards, it's also important to have cash on hand for smaller purchases and to use at markets or street vendors. It's also a good idea to let your bank know that you'll be traveling to Greece to avoid any issues with your credit card.

Water bottle

It's important to stay hydrated during your trip to Rhodes, especially in the hot weather. Packing a reusable water bottle can help you save money and reduce waste by refilling it at public water fountains or cafes.

Insect repellent

Rhodes is known for its mosquito population, especially during the summer months. Packing insect repellent can help you avoid getting bitten and potentially contracting mosquito-borne illnesses.

Camera or smartphone

Rhodes has many beautiful sights and attractions that are worth capturing, so it's important to pack a camera or smartphone to take photos and document your trip. Don't forget to bring extra batteries or a portable charger to ensure you don't run out of battery while taking photos.

Maps and guidebooks

While it's easy to rely on smartphone maps and apps, it's also a good idea to pack physical maps and guidebooks to help you navigate Rhodes and learn about its history and culture. These resources can also come in handy if you don't have access to a reliable internet connection.

Luggage lock

To keep your belongings safe and secure during your trip, it's a good idea to pack a luggage lock to use on your suitcase or backpack. This can help deter theft and give you peace of mind while traveling.

In summary, packing the essential items listed above can help you have a comfortable and enjoyable trip to Rhodes. By packing comfortable shoes, sun protection, lightweight clothing, beachwear, a travel adapter, medications and a first aid kit, cash and credit cards, a water bottle, insect repellent, a camera or smartphone, maps and guidebooks, and a luggage lock, you can be well-prepared for your visit to this beautiful island.

CHAPTER TWO

GETTING TO RHODES

Rhodes is a popular tourist destination and getting to Rhodes is relatively easy, with several transportation options available to visitors.

By Air

Rhodes International Airport "Diagoras" is a modern airport that serves as the main gateway to the island. The airport is located about 14 km southwest of Rhodes town, making it easy to get to the city center from the airport. The airport has several amenities, including shops, restaurants, and car rental services. There are also several transportation options available for visitors to get to their destinations in Rhodes town.

International flights
Rhodes International Airport is serviced by several international airlines, making it easy to get to the island from many parts of the world. Some of the major airlines that fly to Rhodes include British Airways, Ryanair, EasyJet, Lufthansa, Turkish Airlines, and Qatar Airways. Visitors can also book

charter flights to Rhodes, especially during the peak tourist season.

Domestic flights

Several airlines operate domestic flights to Rhodes from Athens, Thessaloniki, and other Greek islands. Some of the airlines that offer domestic flights to Rhodes include Olympic Air and Aegean Airlines. These domestic flights provide easy and fast access to Rhodes from other parts of Greece, allowing visitors to combine their Rhodes trip with other destinations.

How To Get From The Airport To The City Center

There are several transportation options available for visitors to get from the airport to the city center of Rhodes. These include:

Taxi: Taxis are readily available outside the airport terminal and can take you to your destination in Rhodes town in about 20 minutes.

Bus: The public bus service in Rhodes operates several routes to and from the airport. Bus 23 connects the airport with Rhodes town, while bus 40 connects the airport with the town of Faliraki. The journey takes about 30-40 minutes, and tickets can be purchased from the driver.

Car rental: Several car rental companies operate at the airport, allowing visitors to rent a car and explore the island at their own pace.

By Sea

Rhodes is also accessible by sea, with several ferry companies operating services to the island from various ports in Greece and Turkey. Taking a ferry to Rhodes is a great way to see more of the Greek islands and experience a leisurely sea journey.

Ferries From Athens

Several ferry companies operate daily services between the port of Piraeus in Athens and Rhodes. The journey takes about 15 hours, and there are both daytime and overnight ferries available. Taking the ferry from Athens to Rhodes is a great way to experience a leisurely sea journey and see some of the Greek islands along the way.

Ferries From Other Greek Islands

Rhodes is well connected by ferry to other Greek islands in the Aegean Sea. Some of the popular islands that offer ferry services to Rhodes include Santorini, Mykonos, Crete, and Kos. Taking the ferry from other Greek islands is a great way to see more of Greece and its islands and combine multiple destinations into one trip.

Ferries From Turkey

Rhodes is also accessible by ferry from the Turkish ports of Marmaris and Fethiye. The journey takes about 2-3 hours and is a popular day trip for visitors to Turkey. This ferry journey offers a unique opportunity to experience both Greek and Turkish cultures in one day.

How To Get From The Port To The City Center

Most ferries arrive at the port of Rhodes town, which is located just a few minutes' walk from the city center. The port is a hub for both local and international ferry services, making it a convenient entry point to the island. Visitors can easily walk to their destinations in Rhodes town from the port, as it is located in the heart of the city.

For visitors who have heavy luggage or want to avoid walking, there are several transportation options available at the port. Taxis are readily available outside the port terminal and can take you to your destination in Rhodes town in just a few minutes. The taxi stand is located just outside the main entrance of the port terminal, and visitors can easily find a taxi by following the signs.

Another option for getting from the port to the city center is to take the local bus. The bus stop is located just outside the port terminal, and several bus routes operate from the port to different parts of the island. Bus 1 and Bus 2 both connect the port with Rhodes town, and the journey takes about 10-15 minutes. Tickets can be purchased from the driver or from kiosks near the bus stop.

Finally, for visitors who prefer to explore the island on their own, there are several car rental companies located near the port. Renting a car is a great way to explore the island at your own pace and visit off-the-beaten-track destinations. Some of the car rental companies that operate near the port include Hertz, Avis, and Europcar.

Overall, getting from the port to the city center in Rhodes is easy and convenient, with several transportation options available for visitors to choose from. Whether you prefer to walk, take a taxi, ride the bus, or rent a car, you can easily get to your destination and start exploring this beautiful island.

Getting Around Rhodes

Once you are on the island, there are several transportation options available to help you get around.

Public transportation

The bus service in Rhodes is a cost-effective and convenient way to travel around the island. The buses are air-conditioned and usually run on time. Visitors can purchase tickets on board or from designated kiosks in Rhodes town. The buses connect the main towns and villages on the island, making it easy to get around.

Taxis

Taxis are a comfortable and convenient way to get around Rhodes. They are readily available throughout the island and can be found at designated taxi stands or hailed on the street. Visitors should note that taxi fares are regulated by law, and drivers are required to use a meter. It's a good idea to confirm with the driver that the meter is on before starting your journey.

Car rental

Renting a car is a popular way to explore Rhodes at your own pace. Several car rental companies operate on the island, and visitors can choose from a range of vehicles, including cars, motorbikes, and quad bikes. Renting a car gives visitors the freedom to explore the island's hidden gems, such as secluded beaches and charming villages. Visitors should note that driving in Rhodes can be challenging, especially in the narrow streets of the old town, and parking can be difficult to find during the peak tourist season.

Bicycles

Rhodes is a great island to explore on a bicycle, with several companies offering bicycle rental services. Visitors can choose from a range of bicycles, including mountain bikes, road bikes, and electric bikes. Cycling is a great way to see more of the island and enjoy the beautiful scenery at a leisurely pace. Many of the roads in Rhodes are quiet, making it a safe option for cycling.

Scooters

Scooters are another popular way to get around Rhodes, especially for visitors who want to avoid the traffic and parking issues associated with car rental. Scooters are easy to maneuver in the narrow streets of the old town, and rental companies offer a range of sizes and styles to choose from. Visitors should note that helmets are required by law when riding a scooter.

Walking

Rhodes town is a pedestrian-friendly city, with many of its main attractions located within walking distance of each other. Walking is a great way to explore the old town and soak up the atmosphere of this historic city. Visitors should wear comfortable shoes and be prepared for some uphill walking, especially if they plan to visit the Acropolis of Rhodes or the Palace of the Grand Master.

Boats

Boat trips are a popular way to explore the coastline of Rhodes and nearby islands. Visitors can take a day trip to nearby islands, such as Symi or Halki, or take a sunset cruise along the coast of Rhodes. Boat trips are a great way to see the island from a different perspective and enjoy the beautiful coastline of Rhodes. Visitors should note that boat trips are weather-dependent and may be cancelled in the event of bad weather.

Overall, getting to Rhodes and getting around the island is relatively easy, with several transportation options available to visitors. Visitors can choose to fly to Rhodes, take a ferry from Greece or Turkey, or combine both for a unique island-hopping experience. Once on the island, visitors can choose from several transportation options, including public buses, taxis, car rental, scooter and ATV rental, bicycle rental, and walking.

CHAPTER THREE

ACCOMMODATION IN RHODES

Rhodes has a wide range of accommodation options to suit all budgets and preferences. From budget hostels to luxury resorts, there is something for everyone in Rhodes. Here are some of the best areas to stay in Rhodes, as well as some of the top accommodation options in each category.

Best Areas To Stay In Rhodes

Rhodes is a beautiful and diverse island that offers visitors a wide range of accommodation options. Depending on your preferences and travel style, you may want to consider staying in different areas of the island. Here is a more detailed overview of the best areas to stay in Rhodes.

Old Town

The historic Old Town of Rhodes is one of the main attractions of the island, and staying here will give you easy access to many of the city's top sights. The Old Town is a UNESCO World Heritage Site, and it is famous for its beautiful medieval buildings, narrow streets, and impressive fortifications.

Staying in the Old Town will allow you to immerse yourself in the island's rich history and culture. You can explore the many shops, cafes, and restaurants in the area, or visit the Palace of the Grand Master of the Knights of Rhodes, the Archaeological Museum, or the Jewish Quarter.

Accommodation options in the Old Town range from budget-friendly hostels to luxury boutique hotels. Some of the top choices include the 5-star Spirit Of The Knights Boutique Hotel, the budget-friendly STAY Hostel Rhodes, or the charming Saint Michel Hotel.

New Town

The New Town of Rhodes is the modern part of the city, and it has a more cosmopolitan and lively atmosphere than the Old Town. Staying in the New Town will allow you to be close to many of the island's top restaurants, bars, and shops. It is also the hub for transportation on the island.

Some of the top attractions in the New Town include the Palace of the Grand Master of the Knights of Rhodes, the Acropolis of Rhodes, and the Medieval City Walls. The New Town is also home to several museums, art galleries, and theaters.

Accommodation options in the New Town range from budget-friendly apartments to luxury 5-star hotels. Some of the top choices include the 5-star Mitsis Grand Hotel, the budget-friendly Emmanuel Apartments, or the modern and stylish ibis Styles Hotel.

Ixia

Ixia is a popular resort area on the west coast of Rhodes, known for its long and sandy beach and its excellent water sports facilities. If you are looking for a more active vacation, staying in Ixia might be a good choice.

The beach in Ixia is ideal for windsurfing, kitesurfing, and jet skiing. There are also several schools and rental shops in the area where you can learn or practice these sports. Additionally, there are plenty of restaurants, cafes, and bars along the beach, making it a great place to relax and socialize.

Accommodation options in Ixia range from simple guesthouses to large resort hotels. Some of the top choices include the 5-star Sheraton Rhodes Resort, the budget-friendly Kahlua Hotel Apartments, or the beautiful and luxurious Amathus Beach Hotel.

Faliraki

Faliraki is a lively and popular resort town on the east coast of Rhodes, known for its beautiful beaches, vibrant nightlife, and family-friendly attractions. If you are looking for a lively and entertaining vacation, staying in Faliraki might be a good choice.

The beach in Faliraki is one of the best on the island, with clear waters and soft sand. There are also plenty of water sports facilities in the area, as well as a water park and a go-kart track. In the evening, the town comes to life with its many bars, clubs, and restaurants.

Accommodation options in Faliraki range from budget-friendly apartments to luxury 5-star hotels. Some of the top choices include the 5-star Mitsis Faliraki Beach Hotel, the budget-friendly Faliraki Dream Studios & Apartments, or the beautiful and modern Esperos Village Blue & Spa.

Lindos

Lindos is a beautiful and picturesque town on the east coast of Rhodes, known for its whitewashed houses, narrow streets, and ancient Acropolis. If you are looking for a more peaceful and romantic vacation, staying in Lindos might be a good choice.

The town is built around a beautiful bay with crystal clear waters, and it offers plenty of opportunities for swimming, snorkeling, and sunbathing. The Acropolis of Lindos is one of the top attractions on the island, and it offers stunning views of the surrounding landscape.

Accommodation options in Lindos range from traditional guesthouses to luxury boutique hotels. Some of the top choices include the luxurious Melenos Lindos Hotel, the charming and romantic Lindos Blu Hotel, or the budget-friendly Lindos Sun Hotel.

Kallithea

Kallithea is a small resort town on the east coast of Rhodes, known for its beautiful beaches and its famous thermal springs. If you are looking for a relaxing and rejuvenating vacation, staying in Kallithea might be a good choice.

The town is home to several beautiful beaches, including Kallithea Beach, which is one of the most popular on the island. There are also several spa centers and wellness facilities in the area, where you can enjoy massages, hydrotherapy, and other treatments.

Accommodation options in Kallithea range from budget-friendly guesthouses to luxury resort hotels. Some of the top choices include the 5-star Kresten Royal Villas & Spa, the romantic Kalithea Mare Palace, or the budget-friendly Summer Memories Aparthotel.

Rhodes Countryside

If you are looking for a more peaceful and rural vacation, you may want to consider staying in the countryside of Rhodes. The island has many beautiful villages and small towns, where you can experience the traditional way of life and enjoy the beautiful nature.

Some of the top villages to stay in include Afandou, Archangelos, and Koskinou. These villages offer plenty of opportunities for hiking, cycling, and horse riding, as well as for enjoying local food and wine.

Accommodation options in the countryside of Rhodes range from traditional guesthouses to luxury villas. Some of the top choices include the charming Elefteria Apartments in Afandou, the luxurious Ktima Lindos Villa Resort in Koskinou, or the romantic Maravelia Villas in Archangelos.

In conclusion, Rhodes offers a wide range of accommodation options for every type of traveler. Whether you prefer to stay in the historic Old Town, the modern New Town, the lively resorts of Ixia and Faliraki, the picturesque Lindos, the relaxing Kallithea, or the peaceful countryside, you are sure to find a place that suits your needs and preferences.

Budget Accommodation Options

Rhodes has many budget accommodation options that are perfect for travelers on a tight budget. These options range from hostels to apartments and provide comfortable and affordable accommodation for those who want to explore the island without breaking the bank. Here are some of the top budget accommodation options in Rhodes:

Hostels

Hostels are a popular choice for budget travelers visiting Rhodes. They offer affordable accommodation options that are perfect for solo travelers, groups of friends, and backpackers. Hostels in Rhodes vary in terms of their location, facilities, and prices, but most offer a range of different types of rooms, including shared dormitories and private rooms. Here are some more details about hostels in Rhodes:

Location

Hostels in Rhodes are located in various parts of the city, but most are located in or near the Old Town. This is a popular area for tourists because it is home to many of the city's historical and cultural attractions. Staying in the Old Town can be a bit more expensive than staying in other areas, but it is worth it for the convenience and proximity to the main sights.

Facilities

Most hostels in Rhodes offer a range of facilities that are designed to make your stay as comfortable and enjoyable as possible. These may include:

Free Wi-Fi: All hostels in Rhodes offer free Wi-Fi, which is essential for staying connected with family and friends back home.

Communal spaces: Hostels often have communal spaces, such as kitchens, living rooms, and outdoor terraces, where guests can socialize and relax.

Lockers: Most hostels offer lockers or storage facilities where you can keep your belongings safe while you are out exploring.

Breakfast: Some hostels offer breakfast as part of their accommodation package, which can be a great way to start the day without spending extra money.

Laundry facilities: Some hostels have laundry facilities available, which can be handy if you are traveling for an extended period of time.

Types Of Rooms

Hostels in Rhodes offer a range of different types of rooms to suit different needs and budgets. These may include:

Dormitory-style rooms: These are shared rooms with multiple beds, typically four to eight, and shared bathroom facilities.

Private rooms: These are rooms that are not shared with other guests and can range in size from single rooms to family rooms.

En-suite rooms: These are private rooms with their own bathroom facilities.

Mixed or single-sex rooms: Hostels may offer both mixed and single-sex dormitory-style rooms.

Prices

Hostels in Rhodes vary in price depending on their location, facilities, and the type of room you choose. Prices for dormitory-style rooms typically range from €10 to €30 per night, while private rooms can range from €30 to €80 per night. Prices are generally higher in the peak summer season and lower during the shoulder and off-seasons.

In summary, hostels in Rhodes offer a range of affordable accommodation options for budget travelers. They are typically located in or near the Old Town and offer a range of facilities, such as free Wi-Fi, communal spaces, lockers, and breakfast. Hostels offer a range of different types of rooms, including dormitory-style rooms, private rooms, and en-suite rooms, to suit different needs and budgets. Prices vary depending on the type of room and season.

Guesthouses

Guesthouses are a great accommodation option for budget-conscious travelers who want to experience a more personal and authentic side of Rhodes. These small, family-run properties offer a chance to stay in traditional Greek homes and neighborhoods, away from the hustle and bustle of the tourist crowds. Here are some more details about guesthouses in Rhodes:

Location

Guesthouses in Rhodes are typically located in residential areas, often in traditional villages or smaller towns away from the main tourist centers. This provides an opportunity for guests to experience local life and culture, as well as a more peaceful and relaxed atmosphere. Some guesthouses are located in the countryside or near the beach, offering a chance to enjoy the natural beauty of Rhodes.

Accommodation

Guesthouses in Rhodes come in a range of sizes and styles, from small family-run houses to larger properties with multiple rooms. Most guesthouses offer private rooms with en-suite bathrooms, although some may have shared bathrooms. The rooms are typically furnished in a traditional Greek style, with simple but comfortable beds and basic amenities.

Facilities
Guesthouses in Rhodes may offer a range of facilities depending on the property. Some guesthouses have gardens or outdoor spaces where guests can relax and enjoy the sunshine. Others may have communal areas for guests to socialize or a small kitchenette where guests can prepare their own meals. Many guesthouses also offer breakfast, which is often included in the room rate.

Hospitality
One of the highlights of staying in a guesthouse in Rhodes is the hospitality of the owners. These properties are often run by local families who take great pride in welcoming guests and sharing their culture and traditions. Many guesthouse owners are happy to provide advice and recommendations for local activities and attractions, as well as tips for exploring the island.

Examples Of Guesthouses In Rhodes
One of the best-known guesthouses in Rhodes is the Medieval Rose, located in the heart of the Old Town. This charming property offers a range of rooms, each with its own unique style and character. The property also has a rooftop terrace with stunning views of the city and a small garden where guests can relax.

Another popular guesthouse in Rhodes is Archangelos Village, located in the traditional village of Archangelos. This property offers comfortable and affordable rooms, each with a private bathroom and balcony or terrace. The guesthouse also has a beautiful garden and a traditional Greek taverna on-site, serving delicious local food.

In summary, guesthouses in Rhodes offer a unique and authentic accommodation option for travelers looking to experience local life and culture. These properties offer comfortable rooms, personal hospitality, and a chance to stay in traditional Greek homes and neighborhoods. With a range of locations and facilities available, there is a guesthouse in Rhodes to suit every budget and taste.

Apartments

Apartments are a great option for budget-conscious travelers who are looking for more space, privacy, and independence during their stay in Rhodes. Whether you're traveling with a group of friends or family, or simply want the convenience of your own kitchen and living area, apartments are an ideal option for your budget accommodation needs.

Apartments in Rhodes are available in a variety of sizes, from small studios to larger two- or three-bedroom units. They are typically located in residential areas, near the beach, or in the city center. Many apartments also offer stunning views of the Aegean Sea or the charming Old Town.

One of the key benefits of renting an apartment in Rhodes is the ability to cook your own meals. This can save you a significant amount of money on dining out, which can be a major expense when traveling. Most apartments come equipped with a kitchenette or full kitchen, which allows you to prepare your own meals at your convenience. Local markets and supermarkets are also easily accessible, making it easy to stock up on ingredients for meals.

In addition to their kitchen facilities, most apartments also come with a living area, which provides a comfortable space to relax and unwind after a long day of sightseeing. Many apartments also offer amenities such as air conditioning, free Wi-Fi, and cable TV, making them a comfortable home away from home.

When it comes to budget apartment options in Rhodes, Emmanuel Apartments is one of the most popular choices. These apartments are located in the New Town, just a short walk from the beach, and offer simple and affordable accommodations. Each apartment has a small kitchenette, and there are plenty of shops and restaurants nearby. The staff is friendly and helpful, and the apartments are clean and comfortable.

In summary, apartments are an excellent budget accommodation option in Rhodes, offering space, privacy, and the ability to cook your own meals. With a variety of options available, from small studios to larger apartments, you can easily find the perfect apartment to fit your budget and needs.

Luxury Accommodation Options

If you're looking for a truly indulgent stay in Rhodes, there are plenty of luxury accommodation options to choose from. Whether you prefer 5-star hotels, private villas, or all-inclusive resorts, there is something for everyone. Here are some of the best luxury accommodation options in Rhodes:

5-Star Hotels

Mitsis Grand Hotel - This elegant 5-star hotel is located in the New Town of Rhodes, just a few steps from the beach. The hotel has 405 rooms and suites, all of which are decorated in a modern and stylish design. The hotel has several restaurants and bars, as well as a swimming pool, a spa, and a fitness center.

Sheraton Rhodes Resort - This luxurious 5-star hotel is located on the east coast of Rhodes, just a short drive from the city center. The hotel has 401 rooms and suites, all of which are spacious and elegantly decorated. The hotel has several restaurants and bars, as well as a swimming pool, a spa, and a fitness center.

Rodos Palace Hotel - This luxurious 5-star hotel is located in Ixia, just a short drive from the city center. The hotel has 785 rooms and suites, all of which are spacious and beautifully decorated. The hotel has several restaurants and bars, as well as a swimming pool, a spa, and a fitness center.

Villas And Private Homes

Villa di Mare - This luxurious beachfront villa is located in Kallithea, just a short drive from the city center. The villa has 5 bedrooms, all of which are beautifully decorated and have sea views. The villa has a private swimming pool, a large outdoor terrace, and direct access to the beach.

Atrium Prestige Thalasso Spa Resort & Villas - This luxurious resort is located on the east coast of Rhodes and offers a range of private villas and suites. The villas are spacious and beautifully decorated, and each one has a private swimming pool and a large outdoor terrace. The resort has several restaurants and bars, as well as a thalasso spa and a fitness center.

Casa Cook Rhodes - This stylish and luxurious hotel is located in Kolymbia, on the east coast of Rhodes. In addition to its hotel rooms, Casa Cook Rhodes also offers a range of private villas with one to three bedrooms. The villas are beautifully decorated and have their own private swimming pool and outdoor terrace.

All-Inclusive Resorts

Mitsis Faliraki Beach Hotel & Spa - This all-inclusive resort is located on the east coast of Rhodes, in the popular resort town of Faliraki. The resort has 348 rooms and suites, all of which are spacious and beautifully decorated. The resort has several restaurants and bars, as well as a large swimming pool, a spa, and a fitness center.

Labranda Blue Bay Resort - This all-inclusive resort is located in Ialyssos, on the west coast of Rhodes. The resort has 476 rooms and suites, all of which are spacious and modern. The resort has several restaurants and bars, as well as a large swimming pool, a spa, and a fitness center.

Lindos Imperial Resort & Spa - This all-inclusive resort is located in Kiotari, on the east coast of Rhodes. The resort has 462 rooms and suites, all of which are spacious and elegantly decorated. The resort has several restaurants and bars, as well as a large swimming pool, a spa, and a fitness center.

Other Accommodation Options

If you're looking for accommodation that is more budget-friendly or something that is more unique, there are plenty of other options to choose from in Rhodes. Here are some other accommodation options to consider:

Boutique Hotels - If you're looking for something that is a bit more unique, Rhodes has a range of boutique hotels to choose from. These hotels offer personalized service and often have a unique design or theme. Some popular boutique hotels in Rhodes include the Spirit of the Knights Boutique Hotel in the Old Town and the Lindos Blu Hotel & Suites on the east coast of Rhodes.

Camping and Glamping - For those who enjoy the great outdoors, Rhodes has several camping and glamping options available. Camping is a great way to explore the island's natural beauty, and glamping provides a more luxurious camping experience. Some popular camping and glamping options in Rhodes include the Paradise Camping & Glamping in Gennadi and the Glamping Rodos in Kiotari.

No matter what type of accommodation you're looking for, Rhodes has something for everyone. It doesn't matter if you prefer a luxurious 5-star hotel, a private villa, or a more budget-friendly option, there are plenty of options to choose from. Take your time to research and choose the accommodation that best suits your needs and budget, and enjoy your stay in this beautiful island paradise.

CHAPTER FOUR

FOOD AND DRINK

Rhodes is known for its delicious Mediterranean cuisine, which is characterized by fresh and simple ingredients. From fresh seafood to grilled meats, there's no shortage of tasty options to try in Rhodes. In this chapter, we'll explore the local cuisine, best restaurants, and nightlife in Rhodes.

Local Cuisine

Rhodes is a true paradise for food lovers, offering a variety of delicious dishes that are full of flavor and tradition. Greek cuisine is characterized by its simplicity and use of fresh ingredients, and Rhodes is no exception. Here are some of the must-try local dishes that you shouldn't miss during your visit:

Meze Meze: This is a popular way of dining in Greece, especially in the tavernas, where you can enjoy small plates of different appetizers. Meze dishes include a wide variety of options such as tzatziki, stuffed grape leaves, fried calamari, fava beans, and grilled octopus. Meze is usually served with ouzo, the traditional Greek anise-flavored drink, and is a great way to experience the local culture.

Souvlaki: This is one of the most popular Greek dishes that you'll find all over the country, and Rhodes is no exception. Souvlaki consists of small skewers of meat, usually pork or chicken, that are marinated and grilled to perfection. Souvlaki is often served with pita bread, tomatoes, onions, and a yogurt-based sauce, and is a delicious and affordable meal option.

Moussaka: This is a classic Greek dish that consists of layers of eggplant, potatoes, and ground meat (usually beef or lamb), topped with a creamy béchamel sauce. The dish is then baked until golden brown, and served hot with a side salad. Moussaka is a hearty and filling meal that is perfect for colder days.

Greek Salad: This is a refreshing and healthy salad that consists of fresh vegetables such as tomatoes, cucumbers, onions, and peppers, topped with feta cheese and a drizzle of olive oil. Greek salad is a staple dish in Greece and is a great way to enjoy the local produce.

Stuffed Vegetables: This is another popular dish in Rhodes and Greece in general. Stuffed vegetables include a variety of options such as tomatoes, peppers, zucchini, and eggplants, that are hollowed out and filled with a mixture of rice, herbs, and ground meat. The stuffed vegetables are then baked in the oven until tender and served hot with a side of yogurt sauce.

Seafood: With its location on the Aegean Sea, Rhodes is known for its delicious seafood dishes. From grilled fish to fried calamari and octopus, seafood lovers will find plenty of options to choose from. One of the most popular seafood dishes in Rhodes is grilled sea bream or sea bass, served with a side of vegetables and potatoes.

Overall, Rhodes offers a delicious and varied cuisine that is sure to satisfy every palate. Make sure to try some of these local dishes during your visit to experience the best of Greek cuisine.

Best Restaurants In Rhodes

Rhodes is a foodie's paradise, with a plethora of restaurants to choose from. Whether you're looking for traditional Greek cuisine or modern Mediterranean dishes, there's something for everyone in Rhodes. Here are some of the best restaurants in the Old Town, New Town, and on the beach.

Old Town

The Old Town of Rhodes is a UNESCO World Heritage Site and is home to some of the best restaurants on the island. Here are a few top picks:

Mavrikos: Located in a beautiful courtyard in the heart of the Old Town, Mavrikos is a traditional Greek restaurant that serves up fresh seafood, grilled meats, and other classic dishes. The restaurant has a cozy interior for colder days and a charming outdoor seating area for warmer weather.

Tamam: Tamam is a modern Mediterranean restaurant that offers a creative twist on classic dishes. The menu features a great selection of vegetarian and vegan options, as well as gluten-free options. The restaurant has a beautiful courtyard with a relaxing atmosphere.

Marco Polo Cafe: If you're looking for a casual spot for lunch or coffee, Marco Polo Cafe is the perfect spot. The cafe has a cozy interior and a lovely outdoor seating area. They serve up a great selection of sandwiches, salads, and other light bites.

New Town

The New Town of Rhodes has a more modern vibe and is home to a variety of restaurants that cater to different tastes. Here are a few top picks:

Koozina: Koozina is a family-owned restaurant that serves up traditional Greek dishes with a modern twist. The menu features a mix of meat and seafood dishes, as well as vegetarian options. The restaurant has a cozy interior and a lovely outdoor seating area.

Marco Polo Mansion: Located in a beautiful mansion in the heart of the New Town, Marco Polo Mansion is a popular spot for fine dining. The menu features a great selection of Mediterranean dishes, and the restaurant has a beautiful courtyard with a relaxing atmosphere.

Enigma: If you're looking for a more upscale dining experience, Enigma is the perfect spot. The restaurant offers a great selection of seafood and meat dishes, as well as vegetarian options. The restaurant has a sophisticated interior and a lovely outdoor seating area.

On The Beach

Rhodes is known for its beautiful beaches, and there are plenty of restaurants that offer stunning views of the sea. Here are a few top picks:

Kavos: Kavos is a beachfront restaurant that offers stunning views of the sea. The restaurant serves up fresh seafood and classic Greek dishes, and they also offer a great selection of cocktails. The atmosphere is relaxed and laid-back, perfect for a lazy day at the beach.

Mojito Beach Bar: Mojito Beach Bar is another popular spot for beachfront dining. The bar offers a great selection of cocktails and light bites, and they also host regular events and parties. The atmosphere is lively and fun, perfect for a night out with friends.

Symposio Beach Restaurant: Symposio is a beachfront restaurant that offers a great selection of seafood and Mediterranean dishes. The restaurant has a sophisticated atmosphere and a lovely outdoor seating area, perfect for a romantic dinner by the sea.

Overall, Rhodes has a great selection of restaurants to choose from, whether you're looking for traditional Greek cuisine or modern Mediterranean dishes. Don't miss out on the chance to try some of the island's delicious cuisine during your stay.

Nightlife In Rhodes

Nightlife in Rhodes is vibrant and varied, with plenty of options to suit every taste and budget. From cozy bars in the Old Town to beach bars and clubs along the coast, there's something for everyone. In this section, we'll explore the different types of nightlife options available in Rhodes.

Bars And Clubs In The Old Town

The Old Town of Rhodes is known for its charming atmosphere and historic architecture, but it also has a lively nightlife scene. There are plenty of bars and clubs in the area, ranging from cozy tavernas to trendy cocktail bars. Here are a few top picks:

Arionos Square: This lively square in the heart of the Old Town is a popular spot for locals and tourists alike. It's surrounded by bars and cafes that spill out onto the cobblestone streets. It's a great spot to people-watch and soak up the atmosphere.

Kavala Bar: This cozy bar in the heart of the Old Town is known for its great cocktails and friendly staff. It's a popular spot for pre-dinner drinks or a nightcap.

Laganis: This popular nightclub in the Old Town attracts a young crowd and is known for its great music and lively atmosphere. It's open until the early hours of the morning, making it a popular spot for night owls.

Bars And Clubs In The New Town

The New Town of Rhodes is a more modern area, with plenty of bars and clubs to choose from. Here are a few top picks:

Colorado Club: This popular club in the New Town is known for its great music and lively atmosphere. The club hosts regular DJ nights and attracts a young crowd.

Berlin Bar: This trendy bar in the New Town is known for its great cocktails and industrial-chic decor. It's a popular spot for a night out with friends.

Guava Beach Bar: This beachfront bar in the New Town offers stunning views of the sea and is a popular spot for a sunset drink. It's known for its relaxed atmosphere and great cocktails.

Beach Bars And Clubs

Rhodes is known for its beautiful beaches, and there are plenty of beach bars and clubs along the coast. Here are a few top picks:

Mojito Beach Bar: If you're looking for a beach bar with great cocktails and a relaxed vibe, Mojito Beach Bar is the place to go. The bar is located on Elli Beach and offers stunning views of the sea.

Kavos: If you're looking for a beachfront restaurant with stunning views, Kavos is the perfect spot. The restaurant serves fresh seafood and Greek cuisine, and also offers a great selection of cocktails.

Tamam Beach Bar: This beach bar in the New Town is known for its great music and lively atmosphere. It's a popular spot for a night out with friends, and often hosts live music events and DJ nights.

Overall, Rhodes has a great nightlife scene, with plenty of options to suit every taste and budget. Whether you're looking for a cozy bar in the Old Town, a trendy club in the New Town, or a beach bar with stunning views, Rhodes won't disappoint.

CHAPTER FIVE

ATTRACTIONS AND ACTIVITIES

Rhodes, Greece is an island rich in history and natural beauty. From its medieval Old Town to its stunning beaches and ancient ruins, there is no shortage of attractions and activities for visitors to enjoy. In this chapter, we will explore some of the top attractions and activities to experience in Rhodes.

Old Town Of Rhodes

The Old Town of Rhodes is a UNESCO World Heritage Site and one of the best-preserved medieval towns in Europe. With its narrow cobblestone streets, impressive fortifications, and historic buildings, a visit to the Old Town is like taking a step back in time. Some of the top attractions within the Old Town include the Palace of the Grand Master of the Knights of Rhodes, the Archaeological Museum of Rhodes, and the Street of the Knights.

Palace Of The Grand Master Of The Knights Of Rhodes

The Palace of the Grand Master of the Knights of Rhodes, also known as the Kastello, is one of the most iconic attractions in Rhodes. The castle was built in the 14th century by the Knights of St. John as their headquarters during their rule over the island. Over the centuries, the castle has seen numerous battles and has been occupied by various groups, including the Ottomans and the Italians.

The castle was partially destroyed in 1856 when a gunpowder magazine exploded, but it was later restored by the Italian government in the early 20th century. Today, the Palace of the Grand Master is one of the most impressive examples of medieval architecture in Greece.

Visitors to the palace can explore its many halls and courtyards, which are filled with medieval artifacts and works of art. The palace's interior has been restored to its former glory, with beautiful frescoes, tapestries, and furniture on display throughout the castle. Some of the highlights of the palace include the Great Hall, which features a stunning vaulted ceiling and beautiful mosaic floors, and the Armor Room, which houses an impressive collection of medieval armor and weapons.

One of the most impressive features of the Palace of the Grand Master is its defensive fortifications. The castle's walls are nearly 7 meters thick in some places, and visitors can walk along the battlements to enjoy stunning views of the surrounding area. The castle's towers and ramparts offer a glimpse into the strategic importance of the castle during the Middle Ages.

In addition to its historical significance, the Palace of the Grand Master also plays an important role in modern Greek culture. The castle is the site of numerous cultural events throughout the year, including concerts, theater performances, and art exhibitions. The castle's beautiful courtyards and gardens are also popular venues for weddings and other special events.

Overall, a visit to the Palace of the Grand Master of the Knights of Rhodes is a must for anyone visiting the island. Its impressive architecture, fascinating history, and stunning views make it one of the most memorable attractions in Greece.

Archaeological Museum Of Rhodes

The Archaeological Museum of Rhodes is one of the most important museums in Greece and a must-see attraction for anyone visiting the island. It is located within the Old Town of Rhodes, in the medieval Hospital of the Knights, and it houses a vast collection of artifacts from the island's rich history.

The museum's exhibits cover a wide range of periods, from prehistoric times to the Byzantine era. The prehistoric section includes artifacts from the Neolithic and Bronze Ages, such as pottery, tools, and weapons. The Classical period is represented by a large collection of statues and sculptures, including the famous Aphrodite of Rhodes.

The Hellenistic and Roman periods are also well-represented in the museum's exhibits. Visitors can see a variety of mosaics, statues, and other artifacts from this time, including the impressive marble statue of Helios, the god of the sun, which was found at the Acropolis of Rhodes.

The museum also has an extensive collection of artifacts from the early Christian period, including mosaics and frescoes from various churches and monasteries on the island. The Byzantine period is represented by a collection of icons and other religious artifacts.

In addition to the permanent exhibits, the Archaeological Museum of Rhodes also hosts temporary exhibitions throughout the year. These exhibitions cover a variety of topics related to the island's history and culture, and they provide visitors with a unique and informative experience.

Overall, the Archaeological Museum of Rhodes is a must-visit attraction for anyone interested in the island's rich history and culture. With its impressive collection of artifacts and informative exhibits, the museum offers visitors a glimpse into the past and a deeper understanding of the island's heritage.

Street Of The Knights

The Street of the Knights is one of the top attractions within the Old Town of Rhodes. This cobblestone street was once the main artery of the medieval town and is lined with impressive buildings that once housed the knights of the Order of St. John.

The street is approximately 600 meters long and leads from the Palace of the Grand Master to the Hospital of the Knights. It is one of the best-preserved examples of Gothic architecture in Europe, and its buildings have been well-preserved over the centuries.

The buildings that line the Street of the Knights were constructed in the 15th century by the knights of the Order of St. John, who were tasked with defending the island against the Ottoman Turks. Each building was designed to house a different "tongue" of the order, with each tongue representing a different language group.

Today, many of these buildings have been converted into museums or other public spaces. The most notable of these is the Archaeological Museum of

Rhodes, which is housed in the former Hospital of the Knights. The museum features a wide range of ancient artifacts, including sculptures, mosaics, and pottery, that have been excavated from sites around the island.

Visitors to the Street of the Knights can also admire the impressive architecture of the buildings themselves. Each building is unique, with intricate details and carvings that showcase the artistic skill of the knights who built them. Some of the buildings also feature impressive courtyards and gardens that are open to visitors.

In addition to its historic significance, the Street of the Knights is also a popular destination for dining and shopping. Visitors can enjoy a meal at one of the many restaurants or cafes that line the street, or browse the shops for unique souvenirs and handmade crafts.

Overall, the Street of the Knights is a must-visit destination for anyone interested in the history and architecture of Rhodes. Its impressive buildings and rich history make it one of the top attractions within the Old Town, and its charming cafes and shops make it a great place to spend an afternoon or evening.

Acropolis Of Rhodes

The Acropolis of Rhodes is an ancient citadel that was built in the 3rd century BC. It sits atop a hill overlooking the city and the sea, and it offers stunning views of the surrounding area. Some of the top attractions within the Acropolis include the Temple of Apollo, the Stadium, and the Odeon.

Temple Of Apollo

The Temple of Apollo is one of the most important and impressive ancient sites on the island of Rhodes. It is located within the Acropolis of Rhodes, which is a citadel that was built in the 3rd century BC. The temple dates back to the 4th century BC and was dedicated to the Greek god Apollo, who was the god of the sun, music, and prophecy.

The Temple of Apollo was a massive structure that measured approximately 60 meters long and 30 meters wide. It was built using local limestone and was decorated with beautiful marble sculptures and intricate carvings. The temple was also home to a number of important artifacts, including a statue of Apollo that was believed to be the work of the famous sculptor, Lysippos.

Today, the Temple of Apollo is a popular tourist attraction and a must-visit destination for anyone interested in ancient Greek history and architecture. Although much of the temple has been destroyed over the centuries, visitors can still see a number of impressive ruins, including the remains of the temple's foundation, its columns, and its architrave.

One of the most impressive features of the Temple of Apollo is its monumental staircase, which is made up of three tiers and is decorated with intricate carvings and relief sculptures. This staircase was used by visitors to access the temple's upper level, where they could view the statue of Apollo and participate in religious ceremonies.

Another interesting feature of the Temple of Apollo is the large altar that was located outside the temple's entrance. This altar was used for animal sacrifices and was an important part of the temple's religious rituals.

Overall, the Temple of Apollo is a fascinating site that offers a glimpse into the religious and cultural practices of ancient Greece. Its impressive ruins and stunning location within the Acropolis of Rhodes make it a must-visit destination for anyone traveling to Rhodes.

Stadium

The Stadium of the Acropolis of Rhodes is an ancient sports venue located within the Acropolis citadel. Built in the 3rd century BC, it was used for athletic competitions and events in ancient times. The stadium is one of the best-preserved ancient stadiums in Greece and is a popular attraction for visitors to the Acropolis.

The stadium was constructed during the Hellenistic period and was used for a variety of events, including foot races, wrestling, and other athletic competitions. It was also used for cultural events and festivals.

The stadium has a horseshoe shape and is carved into the hillside, offering spectacular views of the surrounding area. It has a seating capacity of around 30,000 spectators and was one of the largest stadiums of its time. The stadium was built using local limestone and has a central track that measures around 600 feet in length. The track is surrounded by stone bleachers and there are two starting gates at either end of the track.

Visitors to the stadium can walk along the track and explore the bleachers, which offer a glimpse into the ancient sports culture of Rhodes. The stadium is also home to a number of artifacts, including statues and inscriptions, which provide insight into the history of the site.

Today, the stadium is used for occasional events and concerts, and it remains a popular tourist attraction in Rhodes. A visit to the Stadium of the Acropolis of Rhodes is a must for anyone interested in ancient history or sports culture.

Odeon

The Odeon is one of the most important and well-preserved ancient theaters in Rhodes, located within the Acropolis of Rhodes. It is believed to have been built in the 2nd century BC during the Hellenistic period and was later expanded by the Romans.

The theater was used for a variety of performances, including plays, music, and poetry recitals. It could seat up to 800 spectators and was a popular gathering place for the people of ancient Rhodes.

Today, the Odeon has been partially restored, and visitors can explore its impressive structure and seating areas. The theater's most striking feature is its beautiful façade, which is decorated with marble columns and reliefs depicting mythical figures and scenes from Greek mythology.

Visitors to the Odeon can also enjoy stunning views of the city and the sea from the theater's elevated position on the hill. The site is easily accessible and is located just a short walk from the other ancient ruins within the Acropolis of Rhodes.

Overall, the Odeon is a must-visit attraction for anyone interested in ancient Greek history and culture. Its impressive structure, beautiful façade, and stunning location make it one of the most popular destinations on the island of Rhodes.

Lindos Acropolis

The Lindos Acropolis is another ancient citadel that is located on the eastern side of the island. It dates back to the 4th century BC and is home to a number of impressive ruins, including the Temple of Athena Lindia and the Hellenistic stoa. The site is also home to St. Paul's Bay, which is one of the most beautiful beaches on the island.

Temple Of Athena Lindia

The Temple of Athena Lindia, also known as the Lindos Acropolis, is an ancient temple located on the eastern side of Rhodes. It is situated atop a hill overlooking the town of Lindos and the sea, and it is one of the most impressive and well-preserved ancient temples in Greece.

The temple dates back to the 4th century BC and was dedicated to Athena Lindia, the goddess of wisdom and warfare. It was built in the Doric style and features a number of impressive architectural elements, including 23 columns and a large central cella, or shrine.

Visitors to the Temple of Athena Lindia can explore the site's impressive ruins, which include the temple itself, a Hellenistic stoa, and a number of other structures. The temple is notable for its ornate frieze, which depicts a series of mythological scenes and is considered one of the finest examples of ancient Greek sculpture.

One of the most impressive features of the Temple of Athena Lindia is its location. Perched high atop a hill, the temple offers stunning views of the surrounding area, including the town of Lindos and the sparkling sea beyond. Visitors can also explore the nearby Lindos Acropolis, which is home to a number of other ancient ruins and offers even more breathtaking views.

Overall, the Temple of Athena Lindia is a must-visit destination for anyone interested in ancient Greek history and architecture. With its impressive ruins, stunning views, and rich cultural significance, it is one of the most iconic and memorable attractions on the island of Rhodes.

St. Paul's Bay

St. Paul's Bay is a beautiful natural harbor located on the eastern side of Rhodes. According to local legend, the Apostle Paul landed at the bay in the 1st century AD during his travels to spread Christianity throughout the Mediterranean.

Today, St. Paul's Bay is a popular destination for visitors to Rhodes. It is a picturesque spot with crystal-clear waters, golden sands, and stunning views of the surrounding hills. The bay is surrounded by towering cliffs, which provide a sense of seclusion and privacy, making it a perfect spot for those looking for a peaceful getaway.

In addition to its natural beauty, St. Paul's Bay also offers a number of activities and attractions. Visitors can explore the ancient ruins of a small church that was built in the 13th century on the site where St. Paul is said to have landed. The church has a beautiful mosaic floor, and it offers stunning views of the bay.

Another popular activity in St. Paul's Bay is swimming and snorkeling. The bay has crystal-clear waters that are perfect for snorkeling and swimming, and there are a number of local companies that offer snorkeling tours and equipment rentals.

For those looking for a more active experience, there are also hiking trails that lead from St. Paul's Bay to the nearby Lindos Acropolis. The trails offer stunning views of the surrounding landscape, and they provide an opportunity to explore the natural beauty of Rhodes.

Overall, St. Paul's Bay is a beautiful and peaceful destination that offers something for everyone. Whether you're looking to relax on the beach, explore ancient ruins, or enjoy outdoor activities, St. Paul's Bay is a must-visit spot on your trip to Rhodes.

Beaches In Rhodes

Rhodes is famous for its beautiful beaches, with crystal clear waters, golden sand, and plenty of sun. From secluded coves to bustling beaches with plenty of amenities, there is a beach for every taste on the island. Here are some of the top beaches in Rhodes:

Elli Beach - Elli Beach is one of the most popular beaches in Rhodes, located in the heart of Rhodes Town. The beach is long and sandy, with crystal-clear waters that are perfect for swimming and sunbathing. There are plenty of sun loungers and umbrellas available for rent, and the beach is well-maintained with clean facilities. There are also plenty of bars and restaurants nearby, making it a great spot to spend a whole day. In addition, the beach is easily accessible, with parking available nearby and public transportation options.

Faliraki Beach - Faliraki Beach is one of the largest and most popular beaches in Rhodes, located on the east coast of the island. The beach is known for its long stretch of golden sand and crystal-clear waters, making it a perfect spot for swimming, sunbathing, and water sports. There are plenty of amenities available, including sun loungers, umbrellas, showers, and changing facilities. The beach is also home to a variety of bars and restaurants, as well as water sports and activities such as parasailing, jet skiing, and banana boating.

Tsambika Beach - Tsambika Beach is a beautiful, secluded beach located on the eastern coast of Rhodes. The beach is known for its stunning scenery, with crystal-clear waters and a beautiful backdrop of cliffs and greenery. The beach is relatively quiet and peaceful, with few amenities available. However, there are a few restaurants and bars nearby, as well as water sports and activities such as jet skiing and banana boating.

Lindos Beach - Lindos Beach is a small, picturesque beach located in the charming village of Lindos. The beach is known for its crystal-clear waters and stunning views of the surrounding white-washed buildings. The beach is relatively small and often crowded, but it is worth a visit for the charming atmosphere and beautiful scenery. There are a few restaurants and bars nearby, as well as amenities such as sun loungers and umbrellas.

Anthony Quinn Bay - Anthony Quinn Bay is a small, secluded cove named after the famous actor who owned the property in the 1960s. The beach is surrounded by stunning cliffs and offers crystal-clear waters that are perfect for swimming and snorkeling. The beach is relatively quiet and peaceful, with few amenities available. However, there are a few restaurants and bars nearby, as well as water sports and activities such as snorkeling and diving.

Kallithea Beach - Kallithea Beach is located just south of Rhodes Town and is known for its impressive architecture and natural beauty. The beach is set in a beautiful bay and features a historic spa complex that was built in the 1920s. The complex has been restored in recent years and is now home to a museum, a restaurant, and a wedding venue. The beach is relatively quiet and peaceful, with crystal-clear waters that are perfect for swimming and snorkeling. There are also a few restaurants and bars nearby, as well as amenities such as sun loungers and umbrellas.

Prasonisi Beach - Prasonisi Beach is located on the southern tip of the island and is a popular spot for windsurfing and kitesurfing. The beach is surrounded by stunning cliffs and offers some of the best wind and waves in the region. The beach is relatively quiet and peaceful, with few amenities available. However, there are a few restaurants and bars nearby, as well as water sports and activities such as windsurfing, kitesurfing, and surfing. The beach is also home to a beautiful lighthouse that offers stunning views of the surrounding landscape.

Stegna Beach - Stegna Beach is a small, peaceful beach located on the east coast of Rhodes. The beach is known for its crystal-clear waters and beautiful surroundings, with green hills and rocky outcrops in the background. There are plenty of amenities available, including sun loungers, umbrellas, and tavernas serving fresh seafood and other local specialties.

Agathi Beach - Agathi Beach is a small, secluded beach located on the east coast of Rhodes. The beach is known for its crystal-clear waters and pristine white sand, making it a perfect spot for swimming and sunbathing. The beach is relatively quiet and peaceful, with few amenities available. However, there are a few restaurants and bars nearby, as well as water sports and activities such as snorkeling and diving.

Afandou Beach - Afandou Beach is a long, sandy beach located on the east coast of Rhodes. The beach is known for its crystal-clear waters and scenic surroundings, with green hills and pine trees in the background. There are plenty of amenities available, including sun loungers, umbrellas, and tavernas serving fresh seafood and other local specialties. The beach is also home to a golf course, making it a popular spot for golf enthusiasts.

Agios Pavlos Beach - Agios Pavlos Beach is a small, secluded beach located on the south coast of Rhodes. The beach is known for its crystal-clear waters and beautiful surroundings, with stunning cliffs and rock formations in the background. There are few amenities available, but the beach is worth a visit for its natural beauty and peaceful atmosphere.

Glystra Beach - Glystra Beach is a small, secluded beach located on the east coast of Rhodes. The beach is known for its crystal-clear waters and stunning surroundings, with green hills and rocky outcrops in the background. There are few amenities available, but the beach is worth a visit for its natural beauty and peaceful atmosphere.

Gennadi Beach - Gennadi Beach is a long, sandy beach located on the south coast of Rhodes. The beach is known for its crystal-clear waters and scenic surroundings, with green hills and rocky outcrops in the background. There are plenty of amenities available, including sun loungers, umbrellas, and tavernas serving fresh seafood and other local specialties.

Pefkos Beach - Pefkos Beach is a small, secluded beach located on the east coast of Rhodes. The beach is known for its crystal-clear waters and beautiful surroundings, with green hills and pine trees in the background. There are plenty of amenities available, including sun loungers, umbrellas, and tavernas serving fresh seafood and other local specialties. The beach is also home to a variety of water sports and activities, such as kayaking, windsurfing, and snorkeling.

Vlicha Beach - Vlicha Beach is a small, secluded beach located on the east coast of Rhodes. The beach is known for its crystal-clear waters and stunning surroundings, with green hills and rocky outcrops in the background. There are few amenities available, but the beach is worth a visit for its natural beauty and peaceful atmosphere.

Overall, Rhodes offers a variety of stunning beaches that cater to every taste, from bustling and popular beaches with plenty of amenities to small and secluded coves that are perfect for a peaceful day in the sun. Whether you're looking for water sports and activities or just a place to relax and soak up the sun, Rhodes has a beach that will suit your needs.

Water Sports In Rhodes

Rhodes is a great destination for water sports enthusiasts as it offers a variety of activities to choose from. Here are some details on some of the top water sports available on the island:

Jet skiing

Jet skiing is a thrilling water sport that involves riding a personal watercraft over the water at high speeds. In Rhodes, jet ski rentals are available at many beaches, and tourists can choose from different rental packages depending on their needs. Some rental companies offer guided tours, while others allow riders to explore the coastline on their own. Jet skiing is an excellent way to see the island's beaches, coves, and cliffs from a unique perspective.

Parasailing

Parasailing is an exciting water sport that combines the thrill of flying with the beauty of the ocean. A parasailing ride involves being lifted into the air while attached to a parachute that is towed behind a boat. In Rhodes, parasailing tours are available at several beaches, including Faliraki Beach and Ixia Beach. Most tours last for around 10-15 minutes, and participants can enjoy stunning views of the island's coastline and the surrounding sea.

Scuba diving

Rhodes is home to some of the best scuba diving sites in Greece, thanks to its clear waters and abundant marine life. Scuba diving tours are available for beginners and experienced divers, and there are several diving centers on the island that offer courses and equipment rental. Some of the top diving spots in Rhodes include the Anthony Quinn Bay, which is famous for its colorful fish and underwater caves, and Kalithea Springs, which boasts a unique mix of sea life and underwater architecture.

Snorkeling

Snorkeling is a popular water sport that involves swimming on the surface of the water while wearing a diving mask and a snorkel tube to breathe.

Snorkeling is an excellent way to explore the island's beautiful coastline and discover a variety of marine life. In Rhodes, there are several great snorkeling spots, including the Aquarium in Rhodes Town, which is home to a variety of fish, octopuses, and even sea turtles, and Lindos Beach, which offers crystal-clear waters and an abundance of colorful fish.

Windsurfing
Rhodes is one of the best destinations in Europe for windsurfing. The island's consistent wind conditions and wide range of spots make it a popular destination for both beginners and advanced windsurfers. Prassonisi Beach is the most famous spot for windsurfing, located at the southern end of the island. It has shallow waters and strong winds, making it perfect for learning or improving windsurfing skills.

Water skiing
Water skiing is a fun and challenging water sport that involves being pulled behind a boat while standing on skis. In Rhodes, water skiing is available at several beaches, including Faliraki Beach and Ixia Beach. The sport is suitable for all ages and skill levels, with instructors available to teach beginners.

Wakeboarding

Wakeboarding is similar to water skiing, but instead of skis, a single board is used to ride the waves. The rider is pulled behind a boat, and they perform tricks and jumps on the wake created by the boat. In Rhodes, wakeboarding is available at several beaches, including Faliraki Beach and Kallithea Beach.

Stand-up paddleboarding (SUP)

SUP is a popular water sport that involves standing on a board and paddling through the water. In Rhodes, SUP is available at many beaches and is a great way to explore the island's coastline while getting a workout. SUP is suitable for all ages and skill levels, and rentals are available at most beaches.

Kayaking

Kayaking is another fun and accessible water sport that is popular in Rhodes. Kayak rentals are available at several beaches, and guided tours are also available. Kayaking is an excellent way to explore the island's hidden coves and beaches and get close to its natural beauty.

Overall, water sports in Rhodes offer something for everyone, from adrenaline-fueled activities like jet skiing and parasailing to more relaxed pursuits like snorkeling and scuba diving. With its beautiful coastline and clear waters, Rhodes is the perfect destination for water sports enthusiasts.

Hiking And Nature In Rhodes

Rhodes is a stunning island located in the Aegean Sea and is known for its beautiful natural landscapes and diverse wildlife. The island is a paradise for outdoor enthusiasts, offering a variety of hiking trails and opportunities to explore the island's natural beauty. From the rugged terrain of the mountains to the pristine beaches, visitors can experience the island's unique flora and fauna while enjoying a range of outdoor activities. Whether you're an experienced hiker or a casual nature lover, Rhodes has something for everyone to enjoy.

Valley of the Butterflies

The Valley of the Butterflies is a natural reserve that is located on the western side of the island. This area is home to thousands of butterflies, including the Jersey Tiger Moth, which migrate to the valley during the summer months. Visitors can walk through the hiking trails that wind through the valley, past the small streams and waterfalls that are fed by the nearby river. The valley is also home to a beautiful waterfall, which is a popular spot for photos. While in the valley, visitors can also explore the small museum that showcases the life cycle and habits of the butterflies that call this area home.

Seven Springs

Seven Springs is a natural area that is located in the heart of Rhodes. The area is home to a small lake and a series of springs that feed into it, creating a tranquil oasis in the midst of the island's dry landscape. Visitors can explore the hiking trails that wind through the forest, crossing wooden bridges and passing small waterfalls along the way. The area is surrounded by lush vegetation, including plane trees and ferns, which provide a welcome respite from the heat of the island's summer sun. The lake at Seven Springs is also a popular spot for swimming and cooling off during the hot summer months.

Profitis Ilias Mountain

Profitis Ilias Mountain is the highest peak on Rhodes, reaching an elevation of 823 meters (2,700 feet). The mountain is located in the center of the island and offers panoramic views of the surrounding area from its summit. Visitors can hike the trail that leads to the top, passing through forests and small villages along the way. The hike is challenging, but the stunning views from the summit make it well worth the effort. At the summit, visitors can enjoy a panoramic view of the island, including the Aegean Sea and the nearby islands.

Filerimos Hill

Filerimos Hill is located on the western side of the island and is home to a monastery and a series of ruins, including a medieval castle and a 2nd-century BC acropolis. Visitors can explore the ruins and enjoy the views from the top of the hill. The monastery is a popular spot for visitors, and the grounds are home to a number of peacocks and other wildlife. There are also hiking trails that wind through the surrounding forests and olive groves, providing visitors with an opportunity to explore the area's natural beauty.

Tsambika Monastery

Tsambika Monastery is a 15th-century monastery that is located on a hill overlooking Tsambika Beach. Visitors can climb the hill to reach the monastery and enjoy the views of the surrounding area. The monastery is home to a small chapel, and visitors can explore the interior and admire the frescoes and icons that adorn the walls. There are also hiking trails that wind through the surrounding hills and offer panoramic views of the coast.

Small Villages and Towns

Rhodes is home to a number of small villages and towns that offer a glimpse into traditional Greek life. Lindos is one of the most popular villages to visit, with its narrow streets and alleyways that lead up to the Acropolis at the top of the hill. The village is also home to a number of small shops and restaurants that offer traditional Greek food and handmade crafts. Haraki is a small fishing village that is located on the eastern side of the island. The village is home to a small beach and a number of tavernas that serve fresh seafood. Koskinou is a traditional village that is located on the outskirts of Rhodes town. The village is known for its colorful houses and narrow streets, which are decorated with mosaics and other traditional artwork.

Overall, Rhodes is a destination that offers plenty of options for those interested in hiking and exploring the island's natural beauty. Whether visitors are looking for challenging hikes or more leisurely strolls, there are plenty of trails and areas to explore. In addition to the locations mentioned above, there are many other natural areas and hiking trails to discover, such as:

Prasonisi

Prasonisi is a unique area located on the southern tip of the island. It is a narrow strip of land that is surrounded by the Aegean Sea on both sides, and during low tide, visitors can walk along the sandy beach that connects the mainland to the small island at the tip. The area is popular among windsurfers and kite surfers due to the strong winds that blow through the area, creating ideal conditions for these water sports.

Epta Piges (Seven Springs) Tunnel

In addition to the hiking trails at Seven Springs, there is also a man-made tunnel that leads visitors through the mountain to a small lake on the other side. The tunnel is dark and can be a bit spooky, but it is a unique and memorable experience for those who are up for the adventure.

Mount Attavyros
Mount Attavyros is the second-highest peak on the island, reaching an elevation of 1,215 meters (3,986 feet). The hike to the summit is challenging, but the views from the top are breathtaking. On a clear day, visitors can see all the way to Turkey and the neighboring islands.

Ancient Kamiros
While not a hiking destination per se, Ancient Kamiros is a fascinating archaeological site that is located on the western side of the island. The site was once a thriving city in ancient times, and visitors can explore the ruins of the city, including the agora, the temple, and the acropolis.

In addition to hiking and exploring the natural beauty of Rhodes, there are also plenty of other outdoor activities to enjoy, such as:

Cycling
Rhodes has a network of cycling routes that allow visitors to explore the island on two wheels. There are routes for all levels of ability, from easy coastal

rides to more challenging routes through the mountains.

Horseback Riding

For those who prefer a more leisurely pace, horseback riding is a great way to explore the island's natural beauty. There are stables around the island that offer guided horseback rides through the countryside and along the coast.

Overall, Rhodes offers a wide variety of attractions and activities for visitors to enjoy, from hiking and exploring nature to water sports, beaches, and more. With so much to see and do, it's no wonder that Rhodes is one of the most popular destinations in Greece.

CHAPTER SIX

DAY TRIPS FROM RHODES

Rhodes is a fantastic base for exploring the Dodecanese islands and the Turkish coast. There are plenty of day trips you can take from Rhodes to explore nearby islands, ancient sites, and beautiful beaches. Here are some of the best day trips you can take from Rhodes:

Symi Island

Symi Island is a charming and picturesque island located just a short ferry ride from Rhodes. It is known for its beautiful neoclassical architecture, vibrant colors, and tranquil beaches. The island is small enough to explore in a day, but there are enough attractions to keep visitors busy for a longer stay.

Symi Town, the island's main settlement, is a beautiful port town with pastel-colored buildings, narrow streets, and charming tavernas. The town is divided into two parts, the lower town and the upper town. The lower town is the main port area, where most of the boats arrive and depart. The upper town, also known as Chorio, is a residential area that is situated on the hill above the port. It features beautiful neoclassical mansions, narrow alleys, and stunning views of the harbor.

One of the island's most popular attractions is the Panormitis Monastery, a beautiful Byzantine monastery located on the southern tip of the island. The monastery is dedicated to the Archangel Michael and attracts many pilgrims throughout the year. It features impressive architecture, beautiful frescoes, and a small museum that showcases the history of the monastery.

Symi Island is also home to several beautiful beaches that are perfect for swimming and sunbathing. Some of the most popular beaches include Nos Beach and Marathounda Beach. These beaches are situated in secluded coves and feature crystal-clear waters, soft sand, and stunning views of the surrounding hills.

In addition to its natural beauty, Symi Island is also famous for its local cuisine. The island's cuisine is based on fresh seafood, vegetables, and herbs. Some of the most popular dishes include Symi shrimp, stuffed squid, and tomato meatballs. The island is also famous for its sweet treats, such as the traditional almond sweets known as amigdalota.

Overall, Symi Island is a must-visit destination for anyone traveling to Rhodes. Whether you're interested in exploring the island's rich history, relaxing on beautiful beaches, or experiencing local culture and cuisine, Symi Island has something to offer for everyone.

Kos Island

Kos Island is one of the most popular day trips from Rhodes, thanks to its beautiful beaches, ancient sites, and lively nightlife. The island is located just a short ferry ride from Rhodes and is a great destination for those who want to experience Greek island life.

One of the top attractions on Kos Island is the Asklepieion, an ancient temple dedicated to the Greek god of medicine, Asklepios. The temple dates back to the 3rd century BC and features impressive ruins, including a beautiful colonnade, a courtyard, and several temples. Visitors can explore the ruins and learn about the history and mythology of the ancient Greeks.

Another must-see attraction on Kos Island is Kos Town, the island's capital. This beautiful town is located on the northeastern coast of the island and is home to several important historical sites, including a medieval castle, a Roman amphitheater, and a Hellenistic agora. Visitors can explore the town's narrow streets, beautiful harbor, and charming cafes and tavernas.

Kos Island is also famous for its beautiful beaches, many of which are located on the southern coast of the island. Tigaki Beach is one of the most popular beaches on the island, thanks to its soft sand and clear blue waters. Other popular beaches on Kos Island include Paradise Beach, Mastichari Beach, and Kardamena Beach.

For those looking for a lively nightlife scene, Kardamena is the place to be. This vibrant resort town is located on the southern coast of the island and is home to several bars, clubs, and restaurants. Visitors can dance the night away or enjoy a drink at one of the many beachfront bars.

Overall, Kos Island offers something for everyone, from ancient history and beautiful beaches to vibrant nightlife and delicious Greek cuisine. It's a great destination for a day trip from Rhodes or for a longer stay on the island.

Marmaris, Turkey

Marmaris is a popular Turkish resort town located on the southwestern coast of Turkey, just a short ferry ride from Rhodes. This town is situated in a beautiful bay surrounded by pine-covered hills, and it's famous for its beautiful beaches, lively nightlife, and rich history.

One of the town's most popular attractions is Marmaris Castle, a medieval fortress that dates back to the 16th century. The castle was built by the Ottomans in 1522 to protect the town from invaders, and it features impressive walls, towers, and a beautiful courtyard. Today, the castle has been converted into a museum that displays artifacts from the town's history, including weapons, coins, and ceramics.

Another popular attraction in Marmaris is the Grand Bazaar, a bustling market that offers a wide range of goods, from spices and textiles to jewelry and souvenirs. This market is a great place to bargain and haggle for goods, and it's a great place to buy Turkish carpets, leather goods, and Turkish delight.

Marmaris is also known for its beautiful beaches. Some of the town's best beaches include Icmeler Beach, a beautiful sandy beach that offers crystal-clear waters and plenty of sun loungers and umbrellas. Another popular beach is Turunc Beach, a quieter beach that's perfect for families and couples looking for a peaceful retreat.

For those who love water sports, Marmaris offers plenty of opportunities for swimming, snorkeling, scuba diving, and jet skiing. The town also has a wide range of boat tours and excursions, including a visit to nearby Dalyan, where you can see the ancient city of Kaunos and the famous Caretta Caretta turtles.

Marmaris also has a vibrant nightlife scene. The town's Bar Street is lined with bars, clubs, and restaurants, and it's a popular destination for young travelers looking for a fun night out. Some of the town's most popular nightclubs include Club Areena and Joy Club, while popular bars include the Havana Bar and the Crazy Horse Bar.

Overall, Marmaris is a great destination for travelers looking for a mix of history, culture, and relaxation. With its beautiful beaches, lively nightlife, and rich history, Marmaris is a great place to explore on a day trip from Rhodes.

Fethiye, Turkey

Fethiye is a charming coastal town located on the southwest coast of Turkey, along the beautiful turquoise waters of the Aegean Sea. The town has a rich history that dates back to ancient times, and it is known for its stunning natural beauty, crystal-clear waters, and impressive historical sites.

One of the town's most popular attractions is Oludeniz Beach, which is known for its stunning turquoise waters and breathtaking views of the surrounding mountains. The beach is located in a protected natural reserve and is known for its calm and shallow waters, making it a perfect spot for swimming, sunbathing, and relaxing. There are also many water sports activities available here, including paragliding, scuba diving, and paddleboarding.

Another popular attraction in Fethiye is the Kayakoy Ghost Town, an abandoned village that was once home to thousands of Greek Orthodox Christians. The village was abandoned after World War I when the Greek-Turkish War forced the Greek population to leave the country. The town features beautiful ruins, including churches, houses, and streets, and is now preserved as a historical monument.

For those who love outdoor adventures, the Saklikent Gorge is a must-visit attraction. This stunning natural wonder is a deep canyon that features impressive rock formations and crystal-clear water. Visitors can explore the gorge by hiking or rafting, and there are also many restaurants and cafes in the area that offer local cuisine and refreshing drinks.

In addition to its natural beauty and historical sites, Fethiye also offers a vibrant nightlife scene with many bars and clubs that cater to all tastes and preferences. The town is also famous for its fresh seafood, and there are many restaurants and cafes that serve delicious local dishes, including grilled fish, meze, and Turkish coffee.

If you're interested in exploring historical sites, relaxing on beautiful beaches, or experiencing local culture, Fethiye has something for everyone. With its stunning natural beauty, rich history, and vibrant culture, Fethiye is a destination that should not be missed.

When planning your day trip from Rhodes, it's important to consider the transportation options and the amount of time you have available. Some day trips, like Symi Island, can be done in a half-day or full-day trip, while others, like Fethiye in Turkey, may require an overnight stay.

In addition to the destinations mentioned above, there are many other day trips you can take from Rhodes, including:

Lindos Village: Lindos is a beautiful village located on the east coast of Rhodes. The village is famous for its stunning Acropolis, which dates back to the 4th century BC. The Acropolis features impressive ruins, including a temple dedicated to Athena Lindia and a beautiful amphitheater. You can also explore the charming village, which features narrow streets, white-washed houses, and beautiful courtyards.

Chalki Island: Chalki Island is a small island located just a short boat ride from Rhodes. The island is famous for its beautiful beaches, crystal-clear waters, and peaceful atmosphere. You can explore the island's charming harbor town, which features colorful houses, tavernas, and cafes. Some of the island's best beaches include Kania Beach and Pontamos Beach.

Bodrum, Turkey: Bodrum is a beautiful coastal town located on the Turkish Riviera, just a short ferry ride from Rhodes. The town is famous for its beautiful beaches, ancient sites, and lively nightlife. You can explore Bodrum Castle, a medieval fortress that dates back to the 15th century. The castle features impressive walls, towers, and a beautiful courtyard. You can also explore the town's vibrant market, which offers a wide range of goods, from spices and textiles to jewelry and souvenirs.

When planning your day trip from Rhodes, it's important to consider the weather and the season. The best time to visit Rhodes is from May to October, when the weather is warm and sunny. However, the peak season can be crowded, so it's important to book your accommodations and activities in advance.

Overall, Rhodes is a great destination for day trips, offering a variety of nearby islands and towns to explore. Whether you're interested in history, culture, or natural beauty, there's something for everyone on a day trip from Rhodes.

CHAPTER SEVEN

SHOPPING IN RHODES

Rhodes is a popular destination for tourists and travelers from all around the world, and shopping is one of the most enjoyable activities to do on the island. Shopping in Rhodes can be a unique experience as it offers a blend of traditional Greek products and modern items, catering to all kinds of interests and preferences.

Popular Shopping Areas

Rhodes is a great destination for shopping enthusiasts, offering a variety of shopping areas that cater to all kinds of tastes and preferences. In this chapter, we will explore some of the most popular shopping areas in Rhodes.

Old Town Of Rhodes

The Old Town of Rhodes is a UNESCO World Heritage Site and is famous for its narrow cobbled streets, ancient buildings, and medieval charm. The town is not only a popular tourist attraction but also a great place for shopping.

Socratous Street

- Socratous Street is one of the busiest and most popular shopping streets in the Old Town, located near the central market.
- The street offers a variety of shops selling jewelry, leather goods, ceramics, and textiles, as well as traditional Greek clothing and accessories such as the famous Greek fisherman's cap.
- You can also find antique shops on this street, where you can find unique and rare items like ancient coins, ceramics, and sculptures.
- Socratous Street is particularly famous for its leather shops, where you can find a range of high-quality leather products like jackets, bags, belts, and wallets.
- The street is also lined with cafes and restaurants, making it a great place to take a break and enjoy some traditional Greek cuisine while shopping.

Ippokratous Square

- Ippokratous Square is located in the heart of the Old Town and is a popular gathering place for both tourists and locals.
- The square offers a variety of shops, cafes, and restaurants, with a focus on jewelry shops.
- The jewelry shops in the square sell unique and beautiful pieces made by local craftsmen,

with a range of styles to suit all tastes and budgets.

- You can also find shops selling handmade lace and embroidery, as well as traditional Greek products such as olive oil and honey.
- Ippokratous Square is a great place to soak up the medieval atmosphere of the Old Town while shopping, as the square is surrounded by historic buildings and narrow streets.

Agiou Fanouriou Street

- Agiou Fanouriou Street is a narrow street located in the south part of the Old Town, near the Grand Master's Palace.
- The street offers a variety of shops selling souvenirs, including magnets, postcards, and t-shirts.
- You can also find shops selling traditional Greek products such as handmade soap and herbs, as well as olive oil and honey.
- The street is particularly famous for its pottery shops, where you can find handmade ceramics and pottery in a range of styles and designs.
- Agiou Fanouriou Street is a great place to find unique and authentic souvenirs to take home from your trip to Rhodes.

Aghias Paraskevis Street

- Aghias Paraskevis Street is a narrow street located in the north part of the Old Town, near the Acropolis of Rhodes.
- The street offers a variety of shops selling handmade ceramics and pottery, as well as unique home decor items like lamps, mirrors, and wall art.
- You can also find shops selling handmade jewelry, as well as local food products such as olive oil and honey.
- Aghias Paraskevis Street is a great place to find unique and one-of-a-kind items for your home, or to pick up a special gift for a loved one.

Orfanidou Street

- Orfanidou Street is a narrow street located in the northwest part of the Old Town, close to the Archaeological Museum of Rhodes.
- The street offers a variety of shops selling jewelry, ceramics, and leather products, as well as traditional Greek products like olive oil and honey.
- You can also find shops selling handmade lace and embroidery, as well as clothing and accessories like scarves and shawls.
- Orfanidou Street is a quieter shopping area compared to some of the more crowded streets in the Old Town, making it a great

place to browse and take your time while shopping.

Hippocrates Street

- Hippocrates Street is a narrow street located in the south part of the Old Town, close to the Palace of the Grand Master.
- The street offers a variety of shops selling clothing, shoes, and accessories, as well as traditional Greek products like honey, olive oil, and spices.
- You can also find shops selling handmade lace and embroidery, as well as leather products like bags and wallets.
- Hippocrates Street is a great place to shop if you are looking for stylish clothing and accessories, with a range of shops offering both modern and traditional styles.

Grigoriou Lambraki Street

- Grigoriou Lambraki Street is a narrow street located in the east part of the Old Town, close to the clock tower.
- The street offers a variety of shops selling clothing, shoes, and accessories, as well as traditional Greek products like olive oil and honey.
- You can also find shops selling handmade ceramics and pottery, as well as leather products like jackets and bags.

- Grigoriou Lambraki Street is a great place to shop if you are looking for unique and stylish clothing and accessories, with a range of shops offering both modern and traditional styles.

In conclusion, the Old Town of Rhodes offers a wealth of shopping opportunities, with a variety of narrow streets and covered markets offering unique and traditional products. Sokratous Market, Orfanidou Street, and Hippocrates Street are just a few of the popular shopping areas in the Old Town, each with its own unique atmosphere and selection of shops. Whether you are looking for clothing, accessories, souvenirs, or traditional Greek products, you are sure to find something special in the Old Town of Rhodes.

New Town of Rhodes

The New Town of Rhodes is the modern part of the city and is known for its lively atmosphere and cosmopolitan vibe. It offers a variety of shopping options for visitors.

Mandraki Harbor

- Mandraki Harbor is one of the most popular shopping areas in the New Town, with a variety of shops, cafes, and restaurants.
- It is a great place to shop for souvenirs, as well as high-end designer brands.

- You can find everything from clothing and jewelry to beauty products and home goods.
- The harbor is also a popular spot for boat tours, with many tour operators located in the area.
- Additionally, there are several historic sites and landmarks nearby, such as the medieval walls of the city and the Palace of the Grand Master.

Orfanidou Street

- Orfanidou Street is a pedestrianized shopping street that is popular with both locals and tourists.
- It is a great place to find fashion, jewelry, and accessories, with both local and international brands represented.
- There are also many boutiques selling unique and handmade items, such as handmade leather sandals and jewelry.
- Additionally, there are several cafes and restaurants located along the street, making it a great spot to take a break and grab a bite to eat.

Ermou Square

- Ermou Square is a bustling area located in the heart of the New Town, surrounded by shops, cafes, and restaurants.

- It is a popular gathering place for both locals and tourists, with a lively atmosphere and plenty of things to see and do.
- The square is a great place to shop for souvenirs, as well as local food products and crafts.
- Additionally, the National Theater of Rhodes is located in the square, hosting a variety of cultural events throughout the year.

Rhodes City Market
- The Rhodes City Market is a great place to experience the local culture and shop for fresh produce and local products.
- It is a bustling market filled with vendors selling everything from fruits and vegetables to meats and seafood.
- You can also find a variety of herbs, spices, and other local products, such as honey and olive oil.
- Additionally, the market is a great spot for trying local delicacies and street food, such as gyros and souvlaki.

Overall, the New Town of Rhodes offers a variety of shopping areas to suit all tastes and preferences, with everything from high-end designer brands to local crafts and fresh produce. Whether you're looking to shop for souvenirs, grab a bite to eat, or simply explore the lively atmosphere of the city, the New Town has something for everyone.

Souvenirs To Buy In Rhodes

Rhodes is a beautiful island with a rich history and culture, which makes it an ideal destination for souvenir shopping. From traditional Greek jewelry to handmade ceramics and leather goods, there are plenty of unique and authentic products to choose from. Here are some of the most popular souvenirs to buy in Rhodes:

Jewelry
Greek jewelry is famous for its intricate designs and quality craftsmanship. You can find traditional Greek jewelry made of gold, silver, or bronze, featuring symbols such as the evil eye, Greek keys, and the double-headed eagle. Modern jewelry designs are also available, featuring colorful gemstones and contemporary designs.

Leather goods
Rhodes is famous for its high-quality leather products, such as bags, wallets, jackets, and coats. You can find leather goods made of sheepskin, calfskin, and cowhide, in various colors and designs. Many shops offer handmade leather products, which are unique and of high quality.

Textiles

Textiles such as clothing, rugs, and carpets are also popular souvenirs to buy in Rhodes. You can find traditional Greek clothing such as embroidered blouses, skirts, and dresses. Handmade rugs and carpets featuring traditional designs are also available, as well as modern designs with bright colors.

Local food products

If you're a foodie, you'll love the local food products in Rhodes. Olive oil is one of the most popular products, as Rhodes is known for producing high-quality olive oil. Honey is also popular, especially the pine honey produced in the mountainous regions of the island. Wine is another popular product, with many local wineries producing delicious wines. You can also find a variety of herbs and spices, such as oregano, thyme, and rosemary.

Handmade ceramics and pottery

Ceramics and pottery are also popular souvenirs to buy in Rhodes. You can find handmade plates, bowls, vases, and other decorative items featuring traditional Greek designs. Many shops offer personalized pottery, where you can have your name or a special message written on the item.

Handmade lace and embroidery

Lace and embroidery are traditional handicrafts in Rhodes, and you can find many shops offering handmade lace and embroidery products. You can find tablecloths, napkins, handkerchiefs, and other decorative items featuring intricate lace and embroidery designs.

When shopping for souvenirs in Rhodes, it's important to look for quality and authenticity. Make sure to buy from reputable shops and look for signs of quality such as handmade details, high-quality materials, and attention to detail. By buying local products and supporting local businesses, you can bring back unique and authentic souvenirs from your trip to Rhodes.

Shopping Tips In Rhodes

When visiting Rhodes, shopping can be an enjoyable experience, especially if you're looking for unique local products and souvenirs to bring back home. However, it's important to keep in mind some shopping tips to help you make the most out of your shopping experience.

Bargaining

Bargaining is common in markets and smaller shops in Rhodes. However, it's important to be polite and respectful when bargaining. If you're interested in an item but think the price is too high, feel free to negotiate with the seller. Keep in mind that some items, especially locally made or unique products, may not be negotiable.

Opening hours
Most shops in Rhodes open at 9 am and close at 9 pm, with a midday break from 1 pm to 5 pm. However, some shops may close on Sundays or Mondays. It's always a good idea to check the opening hours of the shops you want to visit in advance to avoid disappointment.

Tax-free shopping
Non-EU citizens can claim a VAT refund on purchases over €50. To do so, you must look for stores that display a Tax-Free Shopping sign and ask for a Tax-Free form. Make sure to fill out the form correctly, and show it along with the purchased item, your passport, and travel documents at the airport or port customs office to receive your refund.

Payment methods
Credit cards are widely accepted in Rhodes, but it's always good to carry some cash. Euros are the official currency in Rhodes, and it's a good idea to exchange some money before your trip or withdraw money from an ATM. Keep in mind that some small shops and markets may only accept cash payments.

Quality and authenticity

When shopping for local products and souvenirs, it's important to look for quality and authenticity. Make sure to buy from reputable shops and look for signs of quality such as handmade details, high-quality materials, and attention to detail. For example, if you're looking for olive oil, look for locally produced olive oil with a high percentage of cold-pressed extra virgin olive oil.

Local customs and etiquette
In Rhodes, it's important to be polite and respectful when shopping. Avoid touching items or haggling aggressively. If you're interested in an item, ask the seller politely for more information or to try it on if it's clothing or jewelry. When buying from markets, avoid touching food items with your hands and use the provided tongs or gloves instead.

By following these shopping tips, you can make the most out of your shopping experience in Rhodes while supporting local businesses and bringing back unique souvenirs and products.

CHAPTER EIGHT

CULTURE AND HISTORY

Rhodes is a fascinating island that is rich in culture and history. Its strategic location in the Aegean Sea made it a coveted prize for various empires throughout history, resulting in a diverse range of influences that are still evident in the island's architecture, cuisine, and traditions.

Museums In Rhodes

Rhodes is home to several museums that showcase the island's rich cultural heritage, ranging from ancient artifacts to modern art. Here are some more details about the museums in Rhodes:

Archaeological Museum Of Rhodes

The Archaeological Museum of Rhodes is one of the most important archaeological museums in Greece, and it is a must-visit attraction for anyone interested in history and archaeology. The museum is located in the restored medieval Hospital of the Knights of Saint John, which is an architectural masterpiece in itself.

The museum's collection covers the entire history of Rhodes, from the prehistoric period to the end of the medieval era. The exhibits are arranged in four galleries that showcase different periods in the island's history. The first gallery displays objects from the prehistoric period to the end of the Mycenaean era, including figurines, pottery, and tools. The second gallery is dedicated to the Hellenistic period, and it includes stunning marble statues, mosaics, and vases.

The third gallery showcases the Roman period, and it includes exhibits such as the Hellenistic and Roman sculptures, architectural fragments, and inscriptions. One of the highlights of this gallery is the mosaic floor from the villa of Dionysus in Koskinou, which dates back to the 3rd century AD.

The fourth and final gallery highlights the history of the city of Rhodes from the medieval period to modern times. This gallery includes exhibits from the medieval period, such as coats of arms, suits of armor, and weapons. The most famous exhibit in this gallery is the statue of Aphrodite of Rhodes, which is made of Parian marble and is considered one of the most beautiful statues of the ancient world.

In addition to its permanent collection, the museum also hosts temporary exhibitions and educational programs throughout the year. The museum's staff is knowledgeable and friendly, and they are always happy to answer any questions visitors may have.

Overall, the Archaeological Museum of Rhodes is a fascinating museum that offers a glimpse into the rich and diverse history of the island. Visitors can easily spend several hours exploring the museum's exhibits and learning about the island's past.

Museum Of Modern Greek Art

The Museum of Modern Greek Art is one of the most important art museums in Greece and is housed in the Villa des Roses, a 19th-century neoclassical building in Rhodes Town. The museum was established in 1982 and is dedicated to the collection, preservation, and exhibition of modern Greek art from the 19th and 20th centuries.

The museum's collection includes over 3,000 works of art, including paintings, sculptures, prints, and drawings. The collection covers a wide range of art movements, including Impressionism, Expressionism, Surrealism, and Abstract art, and includes works by many of Greece's most important artists, such as Nikos Hadjikyriakos-Ghika, Yannis Tsarouchis, and Spyros Vassiliou.

The museum's permanent collection is displayed in several galleries, which are organized thematically and chronologically. The galleries showcase the development of modern Greek art over time, from the early 19th century to the present day. The museum also hosts temporary exhibitions and cultural events throughout the year, including lectures, concerts, and film screenings.

In addition to its exhibitions, the Museum of Modern Greek Art also has an extensive educational program for children and adults. The museum offers workshops, guided tours, and educational activities that are designed to engage visitors with the artworks on display and to promote an understanding of modern Greek art and culture.

The museum's building, Villa des Roses, is a work of art in itself. The neoclassical building was designed by Italian architect Pietro Arrigoni in the 19th century and was the residence of the Italian Governor during the Italian occupation of the island. The building has been restored to its original splendor, with elegant interiors, beautiful gardens, and stunning views of the harbor.

Visiting the Museum of Modern Greek Art is a must for anyone interested in Greek culture and art. The museum's collection is a testament to the richness and diversity of modern Greek art, and the building itself is a beautiful example of neoclassical architecture.

Palace Of The Grand Master Of The Knights Of Rhodes

The Palace of the Grand Master of the Knights of Rhodes is an impressive castle located in the heart of the old town of Rhodes. It was built in the 14th century by the Knights of Rhodes and was the residence of the Grand Master of the Knights. After the Knights were expelled from the island, the castle was used as a palace by the Ottoman Empire and later as a prison. In 1937, the Italian Government restored the castle and turned it into a museum.

The castle's architecture and interior design are impressive, with massive walls, towers, and impressive courtyards. The castle's façade is decorated with sculptures and coats of arms of the Grand Masters, and the interior is adorned with frescoes, sculptures, and ornamental features. The castle has several courtyards, each with its own style and purpose. The central courtyard is the most impressive and is surrounded by galleries that were used for ceremonies and receptions. The courtyard is paved with white and black marble and is decorated with sculptures and fountains.

The castle's interior has several rooms that showcase the history and culture of the island. One of the most impressive rooms is the Great Hall, which was used for the official receptions of the Grand Master. The room has a vaulted ceiling and is decorated with frescoes that depict scenes from the

Bible and Greek mythology. The room also has an impressive collection of medieval armor and weapons. Other notable rooms include the Small Hall, which was used for private meetings, and the Chapel of Saint George, which has impressive frescoes and icons.

The castle's museum has a collection of medieval and Byzantine art and artifacts, including sculptures, frescoes, and ceramics. The exhibits showcase the island's rich cultural heritage, including its connections to the Knights of Rhodes and the Byzantine Empire. The museum also has a collection of ancient Greek and Roman artifacts, including sculptures and coins.

Visitors can explore the castle's interior and admire its impressive architecture and art. Guided tours are available, and visitors can learn about the castle's history and cultural significance. The castle is also illuminated at night, making it a popular spot for a nighttime stroll. Overall, the Palace of the Grand Master of the Knights of Rhodes is a must-see attraction for anyone visiting the island of Rhodes.

Folklore Museum Of Rhodes

The Folklore Museum of Rhodes is located in the village of Archangelos, about 30 kilometers from the city of Rhodes. The museum is housed in a traditional 18th-century mansion that has been carefully restored to preserve its original architecture and atmosphere. The mansion itself is worth seeing, with its stone walls, wooden ceilings, and colorful tile floors.

The museum's collection is dedicated to the traditional way of life on the island of Rhodes, and includes a wide variety of artifacts and exhibits. Visitors can see traditional costumes from different parts of the island, as well as embroidery, weaving, pottery, and other objects that illustrate the customs and daily life of the island's inhabitants. The museum's exhibits are arranged in several rooms, each with its own theme.

One of the most interesting exhibits is the reconstructed kitchen, which showcases the traditional tools and utensils used in cooking and food preparation. Visitors can see a wood-burning stove, a water jug, a bread oven, and other items that were used in everyday life. The living room exhibit is also worth seeing, with its traditional furniture, carpets, and decorations.

Another highlight of the museum is the exhibit on traditional music and dance. Visitors can learn about the different types of music and dance that are still performed on the island, and see traditional instruments such as the lyre and the mandolin. The museum also hosts regular performances and workshops on traditional music and dance.

The museum's workshop is another interesting feature, where artisans demonstrate traditional crafts such as weaving and pottery. Visitors can watch the artisans at work and learn about the techniques and tools used in these crafts. The workshop also sells handmade products, such as woven fabrics, pottery, and other traditional items.

The Folklore Museum of Rhodes is a great place to learn about the traditional way of life on the island and to experience the island's rich cultural heritage. It's a perfect destination for those who are interested in history, culture, and traditional crafts.

Jewish Museum Of Rhodes

The Jewish Museum of Rhodes is an important cultural institution located in the Jewish quarter of Rhodes. The museum is housed in two restored synagogues, the Kahal Shalom Synagogue and the Yanina Synagogue, and is dedicated to preserving the history and culture of the Jewish community on the island of Rhodes.

The museum's collection includes a variety of artifacts and exhibits that illustrate the rich history and culture of the Jewish community on Rhodes. Visitors can view photographs, documents, and religious objects that give insight into the daily lives, traditions, and religious practices of the community. The collection includes items such as Torah scrolls, prayer books, and religious artifacts, as well as personal belongings and household objects that belonged to Jewish families on the island.

One of the most notable exhibits in the museum is a collection of photographs and documents that tell the story of the Jewish community on Rhodes during World War II. During the war, the Jewish community was subjected to persecution and forced to live in a ghetto. The museum has a collection of documents that detail the experiences of the community during this time, as well as photographs that show the ghetto and the people who lived there.

Another important exhibit in the museum is the display of personal objects and belongings that belonged to the Jewish families who lived on Rhodes. These objects provide insight into the daily lives and traditions of the community, and include items such as clothing, jewelry, and household items.

The museum also hosts cultural events and educational programs throughout the year, including lectures, concerts, and temporary exhibits. These events are aimed at promoting understanding and awareness of the Jewish community and its cultural heritage.

Overall, the Jewish Museum of Rhodes is an important cultural institution that provides valuable insight into the rich history and culture of the

Jewish community on the island of Rhodes. Visitors can learn about the traditions, customs, and daily lives of the community, as well as the challenges and tragedies that the community faced during World War II. The museum is a must-visit destination for anyone interested in learning more about the diverse cultural heritage of Rhodes.

Bee Museum

The Bee Museum, located in the village of Pastida, is a small museum dedicated to the history and culture of beekeeping on the island of Rhodes. The museum is housed in a traditional stone house and has several exhibits that showcase the importance of bees in the ecology and agriculture of the island, as well as the traditional methods and tools used in beekeeping.

One of the main attractions of the Bee Museum is its collection of beekeeping equipment, which includes traditional bee hives, honey extractors, and smokers. Visitors can see how beekeepers have harvested honey over the centuries and learn about the different types of hives that have been used on the island.

In addition to the beekeeping equipment, the museum has exhibits that illustrate the life cycle of bees and the importance of bees in pollination. Visitors can learn about the different types of bees that are found on the island, as well as the plants and flowers that they pollinate.

The Bee Museum also has a small botanical garden where visitors can see some of the plants and flowers that are important to the island's bee population. The garden includes a variety of herbs, fruits, and vegetables, as well as other plants that are commonly used in traditional medicine.

Visitors can taste and purchase honey products from the museum's shop, which offers a variety of locally produced honey, as well as other bee-related products such as beeswax candles and honey-based cosmetics.

Overall, the Bee Museum is a unique and informative attraction that provides visitors with a fascinating insight into the history and culture of beekeeping on the island of Rhodes.

Museum Of Decorative Arts

This museum is located in the historic building of the former hospital of Saint Catherine, in the Old Town of Rhodes. The museum houses a collection of decorative art objects from the 16th to the 19th century, including furniture, ceramics, glassware, textiles, and silverware. Visitors can see the exquisite craftsmanship and intricate designs of the objects, which represent various artistic styles from different parts of the world.

Municipal Art Gallery

This gallery is located in the New Town of Rhodes and showcases contemporary art from local and international artists. The gallery has several rooms that host temporary exhibitions, as well as a permanent collection of modern Greek art from the 20th and 21st centuries. The gallery's collection includes paintings, sculptures, installations, and video art, and visitors can also attend various cultural events and educational programs throughout the year.

Museum Of Mineralogy And Paleontology

This museum is located in the village of Embonas and is dedicated to the study and preservation of the island's geological and paleontological heritage. The museum has several exhibits that showcase the minerals, fossils, and rocks that are found on the island, as well as the geological processes that have shaped the island's landscape. Visitors can also learn about the flora and fauna that have inhabited the island throughout history, including extinct species such as the dwarf elephant and the giant deer.

Maritime Museum

This museum is located in the Medieval City of Rhodes and is housed in the 15th-century building of the Knights of Saint John. The museum has several galleries that showcase the island's maritime history and culture, including exhibits on the traditional methods of fishing, boat-building, and navigation. Visitors can see a collection of ancient maps, ship models, navigational instruments, and fishing equipment, as well as learn about the island's relationship with the sea and its impact on the island's economy and daily life.

In conclusion, the museums in Rhodes offer a rich and diverse cultural experience for visitors who are interested in history, art, science, and culture. Each museum showcases a different aspect of the island's heritage and provides a unique insight into the island's past and present.

Festivals And Events In Rhodes

Rhodes is known for its lively and colorful festivals and events throughout the year. These festivals provide visitors with an opportunity to experience the island's culture and traditions, as well as to interact with locals and other tourists. Here are some of the most popular festivals and events in Rhodes:

Rhodes International Festival

The Rhodes International Festival is one of the most popular cultural events in Rhodes, Greece. The festival has been held annually since 1961, and it showcases a variety of artistic performances, including music, theater, dance, and opera. It is a celebration of the cultural diversity of the island and provides an opportunity for local and international artists to showcase their talents.

The festival runs from June to September and takes place in various venues across the island, including ancient theaters, historic buildings, and outdoor spaces. The venues are carefully chosen to provide an intimate and unique experience for attendees, and they add to the overall ambiance of the festival.

The program for the festival changes each year, but it always features a diverse range of performances to suit different tastes. Visitors can expect to see world-renowned orchestras, opera productions, ballet performances, and traditional Greek music and dance shows. The festival also includes performances by local artists, which provides a unique opportunity to experience the culture of Rhodes firsthand.

One of the most popular venues for the festival is the ancient theater of Lindos, which is a stunning setting for classical music and opera performances. The Palace of the Grand Master in Rhodes Town is another popular venue, with its beautiful courtyard providing a picturesque backdrop for concerts and dance performances. Other venues include the medieval castle of Monolithos, which provides a dramatic setting for theater productions, and the beautiful gardens of the Rodini Park, which is perfect for outdoor concerts.

The festival attracts visitors from all over the world, and it has become a cultural highlight of the summer season in Rhodes. It offers an opportunity to experience the rich culture and history of the island, and to see some of the world's best performers in stunning venues.

Medieval Rose Festival

The Medieval Rose Festival is an annual event held in Rhodes Town, which celebrates the island's medieval heritage and the legacy of the Knights of St. John. The festival takes place in May, and it is named after the rose, which was the symbol of the Knights of St. John.

The festival aims to create an authentic medieval atmosphere, and the highlight of the event is the Grand Parade, which features knights, drummers, and flag bearers, all dressed in medieval costumes. The parade winds through the streets of Rhodes Town, passing by important landmarks such as the Palace of the Grand Master of the Knights of Rhodes, and the medieval city walls.

In addition to the Grand Parade, there are many other events and activities to enjoy during the festival. Visitors can attend jousting tournaments,

[134]

archery contests, theatrical performances, and street markets. There are also a number of workshops where visitors can learn traditional medieval crafts such as blacksmithing, weaving, and pottery.

One of the festival's most popular events is the Medieval Market, which takes place in the historic Square of the Jewish Martyrs. The market is filled with stalls selling all manner of medieval wares, from jewelry and leather goods to traditional foods and drink. Visitors can sample local delicacies such as honey cakes and souvlaki, and wash them down with a glass of the local wine.

The festival also features music and dance performances, with musicians and dancers dressed in medieval costumes. The performances include a variety of traditional Greek music and dance, as well as medieval-style music and dance from other parts of Europe.

Overall, the Medieval Rose Festival is a must-see event for anyone visiting Rhodes who is interested in the island's rich cultural and historical heritage. It is a unique opportunity to experience the sights, sounds, and flavors of medieval Rhodes and to learn more about the Knights of St. John and their legacy.

Lindos Music Festival

The Lindos Music Festival is a highly anticipated event that takes place every summer in the beautiful village of Lindos, on the island of Rhodes. This festival has been running since 2000 and has become a popular cultural event not only for locals but for visitors to the island as well.

The festival showcases a variety of classical music performances, with both local and international musicians taking part. The events are held in the ancient amphitheater of Lindos, which provides an unforgettable backdrop for the beautiful music.

The festival program includes a range of musical genres, including opera, chamber music, and orchestral works. Some of the most renowned classical musicians from Greece and abroad take part in the festival, playing pieces from famous composers such as Mozart, Beethoven, and Tchaikovsky.

The amphitheater in which the festival takes place was built in the 3rd century BC, and it is one of the most beautiful and well-preserved ancient theaters in Greece. The amphitheater is situated at the foot of the Acropolis, and it can seat up to 1,800 people. The theater has amazing acoustics, making it a perfect venue for the festival's classical music performances.

Apart from the beautiful music, visitors can enjoy the stunning views of the village of Lindos and the Aegean Sea. The festival is also an excellent opportunity to explore the village of Lindos, which is one of the most picturesque villages in Rhodes. Visitors can walk through the narrow streets of the village and admire the beautiful white houses, blue-domed churches, and the ancient Acropolis.

Overall, the Lindos Music Festival is an event not to be missed, providing a perfect combination of beautiful music, stunning scenery, and Greek hospitality.

Rhodes Carnival

Rhodes Carnival is a lively and colorful festival that takes place in the weeks leading up to the Christian season of Lent. The festival is celebrated throughout Greece, and in Rhodes, it is a particularly vibrant event that attracts visitors from all over the world. The carnival is a time for feasting, partying, and general merrymaking, and the people of Rhodes take full advantage of the opportunity to let loose and have fun.

The Rhodes Carnival typically takes place in February, although the exact dates may vary from year to year. The festival is a celebration of life and joy, and the streets of Rhodes Town are filled with music, dancing, and revelry. The carnival features a variety of events, including parades, costume contests, music and dance performances, and street parties.

One of the highlights of the carnival is the Grand Parade, which takes place on the last Sunday before Lent. The parade is a colorful and festive affair, featuring colorful floats, acrobats, dancers, and musicians. The parade is a celebration of the island's history and culture, and many of the floats are decorated with traditional Greek symbols and images.

Another popular event during the Rhodes Carnival is the Masked Ball, which takes place on the Saturday before the Grand Parade. The Masked Ball is a formal affair, and attendees wear elaborate masks and costumes. The ball is held in one of the many grand hotels or palaces in Rhodes Town, and features live music, dancing, and plenty of food and drink.

The Rhodes Carnival is also a great time to sample traditional Greek cuisine, with many restaurants and cafes offering special menus and dishes. Visitors can try delicious local specialties such as souvlaki, moussaka, and dolmades, as well as fresh seafood and traditional sweets like baklava and loukoumades.

Overall, the Rhodes Carnival is a festive and lively event that is not to be missed. It is a celebration of life, joy, and the rich culture and history of the island of Rhodes. Whether you are a local or a visitor, the carnival is a great opportunity to let loose and have fun, and to experience the warmth and hospitality of the people of Rhodes.

Rhodes Medieval Festival

The Rhodes Medieval Festival is an annual event that takes place in October and celebrates the island's rich medieval heritage. The festival is held at the medieval castle of Monolithos, which is located on a hill overlooking the sea and provides a stunning backdrop for the festivities. The castle itself is an impressive feat of medieval engineering, with high walls, towers, and a drawbridge.

During the festival, visitors can step back in time and experience life in the Middle Ages. The festival features a variety of events and activities, including reenactments of medieval battles, falconry demonstrations, medieval music and dance performances, and traditional crafts such as weaving and blacksmithing. Visitors can also sample traditional food and drink and shop for handmade crafts and souvenirs.

One of the highlights of the festival is the reenactment of a medieval battle, which takes place in the castle's courtyard. The battle features knights in full armor jousting on horseback, archers firing arrows, and foot soldiers engaging in hand-to-hand combat. The battle is a thrilling spectacle that is sure to impress visitors of all ages.

Another popular event at the festival is the falconry demonstration, which showcases the ancient art of training and hunting with birds of prey. Visitors can watch as falconers release their birds, which swoop and soar through the air, catching prey with remarkable speed and agility.

In addition to the events and activities, the festival also features a medieval market, where visitors can shop for handmade crafts and souvenirs. The market is filled with vendors selling everything from leather goods to pottery to jewelry, all made using traditional techniques.

Overall, the Rhodes Medieval Festival is a unique and fascinating event that offers visitors a glimpse into the island's rich history and culture. Whether you're a history buff, a fan of medieval reenactments, or simply looking for a fun and educational experience, the festival is well worth a visit.

In addition to these festivals, there are also many religious and cultural events that take place throughout the year, such as Easter celebrations and traditional Greek weddings. Visitors can immerse themselves in the island's rich culture and history by attending these events and learning more about the traditions and customs of the local people.

Overall, Rhodes is a fascinating destination for anyone interested in history and culture. Its long and complex history, as well as its diverse range of cultural influences, has created a unique and vibrant island that is well worth exploring.

CHAPTER NINE

MY 19 TO DO LIST FOR AN UNFORGETTABLE EXPERIENCE IN RHODES

Rhodes is an island with a rich history, culture, and natural beauty, making it a popular destination for travelers. Whether you're interested in exploring ancient ruins, relaxing on beautiful beaches, or trying delicious local cuisine, Rhodes has something for everyone. In this chapter, we'll share 19 things you should add to your to-do list to have an unforgettable experience in Rhodes.

1. **Visit the Palace of the Grand Master of the Knights of Rhodes:** This medieval castle was built by the Knights of Saint John in the 14th century and later became the residence of the Grand Master. Today, it houses a museum showcasing the history of Rhodes, including artifacts from the Hellenistic, Roman, and Byzantine periods.

2. **Explore the Old Town of Rhodes:** The Old Town is a maze of narrow streets and alleys, lined with medieval buildings,

Byzantine churches, and charming cafes. The town is surrounded by walls and gates, and inside you can find the Street of the Knights, the Archaeological Museum, and the Palace of the Grand Master.

3. **Relax on the beautiful beaches of Rhodes:** Rhodes is home to some of the most stunning beaches in the Mediterranean. Faliraki Beach is a popular destination for families, while Tsambika Beach is known for its crystal-clear waters and fine sand. Lindos Beach is surrounded by dramatic cliffs and offers spectacular views of the Acropolis.

4. **Take a boat tour around the island:** A boat tour is a great way to explore the hidden coves and beaches of Rhodes. You can take a cruise around the island, visit the neighboring islands of Symi and Halki, or take a fishing trip with the locals.

5. **Visit the Acropolis of Lindos:** The Acropolis of Lindos is one of the most important archaeological sites in Greece. The ancient city was built on a hill overlooking the sea, and the ruins include a temple to Athena Lindia, a theater, and a marketplace.

6. **Take a trip to the Valley of the Butterflies:** The Valley of the Butterflies is a

unique natural wonder, where thousands of butterflies gather during the summer months. The valley is a protected area, and visitors can walk along the stream and see the butterflies up close.

7. **Explore the Seven Springs:** The Seven Springs is a natural oasis with a river, waterfalls, and lush vegetation. You can hike along the river, cross the wooden bridge, and explore the dark tunnel that leads to the lake.

8. **Take a hike in the mountains of Rhodes:** Rhodes has a mountainous landscape, and there are many trails that offer stunning views of the island and the Aegean Sea. You can hike to the top of Mount Attavyros, the highest peak on the island, or explore the forest of Profitis Ilias.

9. **Visit the Archaeological Museum of Rhodes:** The Archaeological Museum of Rhodes is home to a rich collection of artifacts from the island's history. You can see ancient pottery, sculptures, and jewelry, as well as exhibits on the island's Christian and Islamic periods.

10. **Try traditional Greek cuisine:** Greek cuisine is known for its fresh ingredients and simple flavors. In Rhodes, you

can try traditional dishes like moussaka, souvlaki, and tzatziki at local tavernas. You can also sample fresh seafood, such as octopus, squid, and sardines.

11.   **Take a wine tour:** Rhodes is home to some excellent wineries, and you can take a tour of the vineyards and sample the island's delicious wines. The sweet Muscat wine is a particular favorite, and you can also try the dry white wine made from the Athiri grape.

12.   **Visit the charming village of Lindos:** Lindos is a picturesque village with narrow streets and white-washed houses. You can explore the ruins of the ancient city, visit the Byzantine church of Panagia, and enjoy stunning views of the sea from the top of the hill.

13.   **Take a dip in the hot springs of Kallithea:** The Kallithea hot springs are known for their therapeutic properties, and the beautiful Art Deco architecture of the spa adds to the charm of the experience. You can relax in the warm waters and enjoy the beautiful surroundings, or take a spa treatment at one of the facilities.

14.   **Go scuba diving:** The waters around Rhodes are rich in marine life and there are

many dive sites to explore. You can see colorful fish, octopus, and even shipwrecks. There are many dive centers on the island that offer courses and excursions for all levels.

15.   Visit the village of Embonas: Embonas is a charming mountain village known for its wine production. You can visit the local wineries and sample the village's famous red wine, made from the local grape variety, Amorgiano. You can also enjoy traditional food and music at the village's tavernas.

16.   Take a tour of the island's historic churches: Rhodes has a rich religious history, and there are many churches and monasteries to explore. The Monastery of Filerimos is a particularly beautiful site, with stunning views and a Byzantine chapel. The Church of the Annunciation in the Old Town is another important site, with beautiful frescoes and an impressive bell tower.

17.   Go on a horseback riding adventure: Horseback riding is a great way to explore the island's scenic landscapes. You can take a guided tour through the countryside, along the beach, or even up into the mountains.

18. **Visit the Tsambika Monastery:** The Tsambika Monastery is a beautiful Byzantine monastery located on a hill overlooking the sea. The monastery is dedicated to the Virgin Mary, and the site is considered sacred by many locals. You can climb the steps to the top of the hill and enjoy breathtaking views of the island.

19. **Take a sunset cruise:** Watching the sunset over the Aegean Sea is a magical experience, and you can make it even more special with a sunset cruise. You can enjoy a drink and some snacks while taking in the beautiful colors of the sky and sea.

Overall, Rhodes offers a wide range of activities and experiences for every type of traveler. From exploring ancient ruins to relaxing on stunning beaches, trying local cuisine, and enjoying outdoor adventures, there is something for everyone to enjoy and create unforgettable memories.

CHAPTER TEN

PRACTICAL INFORMATION

Rhodes is a popular travel destination located in the Aegean Sea. As a tourist or traveler, it is important to have some practical information about Rhodes to make your trip smooth and enjoyable. In this chapter, we will discuss important practical information about Rhodes, including currency and exchange, language, safety tips, tipping, and local customs and etiquette.

Essential Rules And Regulation Visitors To Rhodes Should Know

If you're visiting for the first time or returning for another visit, there are some essential rules and regulations that visitors to Rhodes should be aware of to ensure a safe and enjoyable trip.

Respect local customs and traditions: Rhodes has a rich cultural heritage, and it's important to respect local customs and traditions. Dress modestly when visiting religious sites, and avoid taking photographs without permission. It's also important to be respectful of local residents and their way of life.

Don't litter: Rhodes is a beautiful island with stunning natural landscapes, and it's important to keep it that way. Always dispose of your waste properly and avoid littering on the streets or beaches.

Respect the environment: Rhodes is home to several endangered species, including the Mediterranean monk seal, so it's important to respect the environment. Avoid damaging plants and trees, and don't disturb the wildlife.

Drive safely: If you plan to rent a car or a scooter, it's important to drive safely and follow traffic rules. Always wear a helmet when riding a scooter, and avoid drinking and driving.

Be aware of pickpockets: As with any popular tourist destination, there is a risk of pickpocketing. Be aware of your surroundings, and keep your belongings close to you at all times. Avoid carrying large amounts of cash, and keep important documents like passports in a secure location.

Check the weather forecast: Rhodes enjoys a Mediterranean climate, with hot summers and mild winters. However, it's important to check the weather forecast before planning outdoor activities to avoid any unexpected weather changes.

Be mindful of the siesta: Many shops and businesses in Rhodes close during the afternoon for the siesta, a traditional midday break. Plan your activities accordingly, and avoid loud noises during this time.

Respect the local wildlife: Rhodes is home to several species of wildlife, including tortoises and peacocks. It's important to respect these animals and avoid disturbing them or feeding them.

Follow beach rules: Rhodes is known for its stunning beaches, but it's important to follow the beach rules. Don't litter, avoid loud music or parties, and be mindful of other beach-goers. Additionally, it's important to avoid disturbing the marine life and coral reefs when swimming or snorkeling.

Be respectful of archaeological sites: Rhodes has a rich history, with several archaeological sites that are popular tourist attractions. When visiting these sites, it's important to be respectful of the ancient structures and artifacts. Don't climb on the ruins or touch the artifacts, as this can cause damage.

Use sunscreen: Rhodes enjoys plenty of sunshine, and it's important to protect your skin from the harmful effects of the sun. Always wear sunscreen with a high SPF, and reapply it regularly throughout the day.

Be respectful of locals: Rhodes is a popular tourist destination, and locals can sometimes feel overwhelmed by the influx of visitors. It's important to be respectful of locals and their way of life. Learn a few basic phrases in Greek, and be polite and friendly when interacting with locals.

Be mindful of the water: While the tap water in Rhodes is generally safe to drink, it's important to be mindful of the water when swimming or engaging in water activities. Avoid swallowing seawater, and make sure to stay hydrated by drinking plenty of bottled water.

Be prepared for mosquitoes: During the summer months, mosquitoes can be a problem in Rhodes. Be prepared by bringing mosquito repellent and wearing long-sleeved shirts and pants in the evening.

Use public transportation: Rhodes has a good public transportation system, including buses and taxis. Using public transportation can be a more affordable and eco-friendly option than renting a car or scooter.

Be aware of the dress code: While Rhodes is a relatively relaxed destination, it's important to be aware of the dress code. Avoid wearing revealing clothing when visiting religious sites or conservative areas.

Don't touch stray animals: Rhodes has a significant population of stray cats and dogs, and while they may be cute, it's important not to touch them. Stray animals can carry diseases, and some may be aggressive.

Respect the local nightlife: Rhodes has a lively nightlife scene, particularly in the capital city of Rhodes Town. Be respectful of locals who may live near bars and clubs, and avoid making excessive noise late at night.

Be prepared for the heat: Rhodes can get very hot during the summer months, with temperatures often reaching above 30 degrees Celsius. Be prepared by wearing lightweight and breathable clothing, staying hydrated, and avoiding the midday sun.

By following these essential rules and regulations, visitors to Rhodes can have a safe and enjoyable trip while respecting the local customs and traditions. With its stunning natural landscapes, rich history, and vibrant culture, Rhodes is a destination that is sure to leave a lasting impression.

Visa And Entry Requirements

If you're planning a trip to Rhodes, it's important to understand the visa and entry requirements for your specific country of origin. This chapter will provide an overview of the visa and entry requirements for Rhodes, so you can ensure that you have the necessary documentation and information for your trip.

EU Citizens

If you're a citizen of an EU country, you do not need a visa to enter Greece or Rhodes. You only need a valid passport or ID card to enter the country. Your passport or ID card must be valid for the entire duration of your stay in Greece.

Non-EU Citizens

If you're a citizen of a non-EU country, you may need a visa to enter Greece and Rhodes. The specific visa requirements depend on your country of origin and the length of your stay. Generally, if you plan to stay in Greece for up to 90 days within a 180-day period, you will need a Schengen visa. This visa allows you to enter and exit Greece and other Schengen countries without the need for additional visas.

To apply for a Schengen visa, you will need to provide several documents, including a valid passport, a completed visa application form, a recent passport-sized photo, proof of travel arrangements (such as flight reservations), proof of accommodation in Greece, and proof of sufficient funds to support yourself during your stay. You may also need to provide additional documents depending on your specific circumstances.

Schengen Area

As part of the Schengen Area, Greece allows for free movement between participating countries without the need for border checks. If you're entering Greece from another Schengen country, you do not need to show your passport or ID card. However, it's still important to have these documents with you in case of an emergency or other unforeseen circumstances.

It's important to note that even though border checks are not conducted between Schengen countries, there may still be security checks at airports or other points of entry. You may be asked to show your passport or ID card, so it's important to have these documents with you at all times.

Understanding the visa and entry requirements for Rhodes is an important part of planning your trip. Whether you're a citizen of an EU or non-EU country, or traveling within the Schengen Area, it's important to have the necessary documentation and information to ensure a smooth and stress-free entry into Greece and Rhodes.

Currency And Exchange

Rhodes is part of Greece, which is a member of the European Union. As such, the currency used in Rhodes is the Euro (€), just like in the rest of Greece and other EU member countries. The Euro is a widely accepted currency in Rhodes, and you can use it to pay for almost anything, from meals and souvenirs to transportation and accommodation.

If you are coming from a country that does not use the Euro, you will need to exchange your currency for Euros. There are several options for exchanging currency in Rhodes, including banks, exchange bureaus, and ATMs. Banks generally offer the best exchange rates, but they may also charge a commission or other fees. Exchange bureaus and ATMs are also widely available in tourist areas, and they may offer more competitive exchange rates than banks.

When exchanging currency, it's important to keep in mind the exchange rate and any fees or commissions charged by the provider. It's a good idea to shop around and compare rates before exchanging currency, as this can save you money in the long run. You can also check the exchange rate online before your trip to get an idea of what to expect.

Credit cards are widely accepted in Rhodes, especially in tourist areas. Visa and Mastercard are the most commonly accepted cards, but American Express and Diners Club may also be accepted in some places. It's a good idea to inform your bank or credit card company of your travel plans before your trip, as this can help prevent any issues with card usage while abroad.

In summary, the Euro is the currency used in Rhodes, and it's widely accepted throughout the island. There are several options for exchanging currency in Rhodes, including banks, exchange bureaus, and ATMs. It's important to compare exchange rates and fees before exchanging currency to get the best deal. Credit cards are also widely accepted in Rhodes, but it's a good idea to inform your bank or credit card company of your travel plans before your trip.

Language

Language is an important aspect of practical information when traveling to Rhodes. The official language of Rhodes is Greek, and it is the language spoken by most locals. However, English is widely spoken in tourist areas, and many people who work in the tourism industry are fluent in several languages.

If you are traveling to Rhodes and do not speak Greek, it is recommended to learn some basic Greek phrases to help you navigate the island and communicate with locals. Basic phrases such as "hello" (yasou), "goodbye" (adios), "please" (parakalo), and "thank you" (efharisto) can go a long way in making a good impression on locals and show that you are respectful of their culture.

It is also important to be patient and polite when communicating with locals, especially if there is a language barrier. Speak slowly and clearly, and try to use simple language to make your meaning clear. Locals will often appreciate the effort you make to speak their language, even if it is just a few words.

If you are having difficulty communicating in Greek or English, there are often translation services available. Many hotels, tourist offices, and businesses have staff members who speak multiple languages and can help you with translations.

In summary, while it is not necessary to be fluent in Greek when traveling to Rhodes, learning some basic phrases and being polite when communicating with locals can make your trip more enjoyable and help you better appreciate the local culture.

Safety Tips

Safety is a top priority when traveling, and Rhodes is no exception. While Rhodes is generally a safe place to visit, there are some safety tips to keep in mind to avoid any unpleasant experiences. Here are some additional safety tips to consider:

Be cautious in crowded areas: Crowded areas, such as the Old Town and public transportation, are hotspots for pickpockets. Keep your valuables close to you and be aware of your surroundings.

Take precautions against the sun and heat: Rhodes is known for its sunny weather, but it's important to take precautions against the sun and heat. Wear sunscreen, a hat, and sunglasses, and stay hydrated by drinking plenty of water.

Stay safe at the beach: Rhodes has many beautiful beaches, but it's important to follow rules and regulations to ensure your safety. Be aware of any posted warning signs, and avoid swimming alone or in rough waters. It's also important to stay hydrated and protect yourself from the sun.

Use common sense at night: While Rhodes is generally a safe place to travel, it's important to use common sense when traveling at night. Avoid poorly lit areas, and do not leave your valuables unattended.

Be aware of traffic: Traffic can be heavy in Rhodes, especially in tourist areas. Always use crosswalks and be aware of your surroundings when crossing the street.

Stay informed about weather and natural disasters: Rhodes can experience natural disasters, such as earthquakes or wildfires. Stay informed about any weather or natural disaster alerts, and follow instructions from local authorities.

By following these safety tips, you can have a safe and enjoyable experience in Rhodes. Remember to always be aware of your surroundings and use common sense, and don't hesitate to ask locals or hotel staff for any additional safety tips or advice.

Tipping

Tipping in Rhodes is not mandatory, but it is generally appreciated for good service. Tipping is usually done in restaurants, cafes, bars, and other hospitality industries. It is also customary to tip hotel staff, such as housekeepers and porters.

In restaurants, a 10% tip is a common amount for good service. Some restaurants may include a service charge in the bill, so it's important to check before adding an additional tip. If you receive exceptional service, you may want to consider leaving a higher tip.

When tipping hotel staff, it's important to remember that the amount of tip may vary depending on the type of service provided. For example, if the housekeeper has gone above and beyond to make your stay comfortable, you may want to leave a larger tip. The same goes for porters who have assisted with your luggage.

It's important to note that in some cases, tipping may not be appropriate. For example, if you receive medical treatment or services from a government office, tipping is not expected.

When in doubt about whether to tip or not, you can ask a local or a staff member for guidance. It's also a good idea to carry some small bills or coins for tipping purposes.

In general, tipping in Rhodes is not mandatory, but it's generally appreciated for good service. A 10% tip is a common amount for restaurants, cafes, and bars. When tipping hotel staff, the amount may vary depending on the type of service provided. When in doubt, it's always a good idea to ask a local or a staff member for guidance.

Local Customs And Etiquette

In Rhodes, it is important to be aware of the local customs and etiquette to ensure that you are respectful towards the local culture and traditions. Here are some key points to keep in mind:

Dress Code: When visiting churches or monasteries, it is important to dress modestly. Women should avoid wearing shorts or short skirts, and should cover their shoulders. Men should also dress modestly, avoiding tank tops or sleeveless shirts.

Greetings: When greeting someone, a simple nod of the head or a smile is acceptable. Handshakes are also commonly used, especially in more formal settings. In more informal settings, such as among friends or family, cheek kissing may be used.

Language: While English is widely spoken in Rhodes, it is always appreciated when visitors make an effort to speak a few basic Greek phrases. Saying "hello" (yasou), "please" (parakalo), and "thank you" (efharisto) in Greek can go a long way in showing respect for the local culture.

Socializing: Greeks are known for their hospitality, and it is common to be invited into someone's home for a meal or a drink. If you are invited to someone's home, it is polite to bring a small gift such as sweets or flowers. It is also customary to remove your shoes before entering someone's home.

Religion: The Greek Orthodox Church is an important part of the local culture in Rhodes. Visitors should be respectful when visiting churches or monasteries, and should follow any rules or dress codes that are posted. It is also important to remember that religion can be a sensitive topic, so it's best to avoid discussing it unless you are with close friends or family.

Food and Drink: Greek cuisine is known for its delicious and fresh ingredients, and meals are often enjoyed as a social event with friends and family. It is customary to order multiple dishes and share them among the group. It is also common to drink wine or ouzo with meals. When dining out, it is important to be aware of the dress code, especially in more upscale restaurants.

Behavior in Public: In Rhodes, it is important to be aware of your behavior in public. Loud or disruptive behavior can be seen as disrespectful, especially in more quiet or traditional areas. It is also important to avoid littering or damaging any historical or cultural sites.

Socializing with Greeks: Greeks are known for their warmth and hospitality, and it is common to be invited to social events such as weddings, baptisms, or other celebrations. When attending these events, it is important to dress appropriately and bring a small gift such as flowers or a bottle of wine. It is also customary to dance and participate in the celebrations.

Driving: If you plan to drive in Rhodes, it is important to be aware of the local driving laws and regulations. The speed limit in urban areas is usually 50km/h and 90km/h on highways. It is mandatory to wear seat belts and to have a valid driver's license. It is also important to be aware of the narrow and winding roads, especially in the Old Town area.

Overall, by being respectful and aware of the local customs and etiquette, you can enjoy a more authentic and meaningful experience in Rhodes. Remember to always be polite and courteous, and to take the time to learn about the local culture and traditions. By doing so, you can create lasting memories and connections with the people and places of this beautiful destination.

Emergency Numbers

It's very important to know the emergency numbers in Rhodes in case of any unforeseen situations. Here are the important emergency numbers to keep in mind:

- **Police: 100**
- **Ambulance: 166**
- **Fire Department: 199**

In case of a medical emergency, you can also contact the National Emergency Number (112), which is available in all European Union countries, including Greece.

It's a good idea to keep these numbers saved in your phone or written down in a safe place in case of an emergency. It's also a good idea to have travel insurance that covers emergency medical situations, so you can get the help you need without worrying about the cost.

In addition to emergency numbers, it's important to know the location of the nearest hospital or medical center in case of a non-emergency medical issue. Many hotels in Rhodes also have a list of nearby medical facilities that guests can use in case of an emergency.

Overall, having knowledge of the emergency numbers and medical facilities in Rhodes can help ensure a safe and worry-free trip.

Useful Websites And Resources For Your Rhodes Trip

Rhodes is a beautiful destination that offers a lot to see and do. As a traveler or tourist, it's important to have access to helpful information and resources to make the most of your trip. In this chapter, we will discuss useful websites and resources that you can use to plan and enhance your Rhodes trip.

Visit Greece
Visit Greece is the official tourism website for Greece and provides useful information for travelers

planning a trip to Rhodes. The website offers information on attractions, accommodations, transportation, events, and more. You can also find helpful tips and guides for exploring Rhodes and other parts of Greece.

Rhodes Tourism

Rhodes Tourism is the official tourism website for Rhodes and offers information on the island's history, culture, and attractions. The website provides information on accommodations, restaurants, transportation, and tours, as well as travel tips and useful links for planning your trip.

TripAdvisor

TripAdvisor is a popular travel website that offers reviews, photos, and travel advice from other travelers. You can use TripAdvisor to research accommodations, restaurants, attractions, and tours in Rhodes, as well as get advice and recommendations from other travelers who have visited the island.

Airbnb - Airbnb is a popular online platform for booking vacation rentals, including apartments, villas, and homes in Rhodes. It is a great option for those looking for more privacy and flexibility during their trip.

Google Maps

Google Maps is a useful tool for planning and navigating your way around Rhodes. You can use Google Maps to find directions to attractions, restaurants, and accommodations, as well as to plan your transportation routes. The app also offers helpful features such as real-time traffic updates and public transportation schedules.

Weather.com

Weather.com is a website that offers up-to-date weather information for Rhodes. You can use the website to check the current weather conditions, as well as to plan ahead for your trip by checking the forecast for your travel dates.

Google Translate

While many people in Rhodes speak English, it can be helpful to know some basic Rhodes phrases. Google Translate is a free translation app that allows you to translate text and speech in real-time. It's a great resource for communicating with locals and navigating the city.

Rhodes International Airport

If you're flying into Rhodes, the official website for Rhodes International Airport provides useful information on flight schedules, airport services, and transportation options to and from the airport.

CONCLUSION

Rhodes is a stunning island in the Aegean Sea that offers a unique blend of history, culture, and natural beauty. From the vibrant nightlife and bustling markets of Rhodes Town to the peaceful beaches and ancient ruins scattered throughout the island, there is something for everyone in Rhodes.

As a traveler, it's important to plan ahead and book accommodations and activities in advance during peak season, as Rhodes can get crowded during the summer months. It's also important to pack appropriately for the weather, as temperatures can get quite hot.

One of the highlights of Rhodes is its Old Town, which is a UNESCO World Heritage Site. With its winding cobblestone streets, ancient walls, and medieval architecture, it's easy to get lost in the charm and history of this enchanting part of the island.

For those interested in history and culture, there are numerous museums, monasteries, and ancient ruins to explore. The Palace of the Grand Master of the Knights of Rhodes is a must-see, as it offers a glimpse into the island's rich history under the Knights of Rhodes.

For those seeking adventure, there are plenty of outdoor activities to enjoy in Rhodes, including hiking, cycling, and water sports. The island's beautiful beaches also provide the perfect setting for a day of relaxation and soaking up the Mediterranean sun.

Overall, Rhodes is a destination that has something for everyone. It doesn't matter if you're interested in history, culture, or just want to enjoy the natural beauty of the island, Rhodes is a place that will leave a lasting impression on you.

ON A FINAL NOTE

The information provided in this travel guide is intended for general informational purposes as diligent effort has been made to ensure the accuracy of the information provided. Readers are solely responsible for their own travel decisions and activities and should use their judgment when following the suggestions and recommendations provided in this guide. Note that prices, hours of operation, and other details are subject to change without notice. It is always advisable to check with the relevant authorities, businesses, or organizations before making any travel plans or reservations.

The inclusion of any specific product, service, business, or organization in this guide does not constitute an endorsement by the author. Readers are advised to take necessary precautions and follow local laws, regulations, and customs. The author and publisher of this travel guide are not responsible for any inaccuracies or omissions, nor for any damages or losses that may result from following the information provided in this guide.

Thank you for choosing this RHODES TRAVEL GUIDE, and bon voyage!

Printed in Great Britain
by Amazon